SHAPING POLITICAL DISCOURSE IN CAMEROON

TRANSLATORS, INTERPRETERS, MILITARY AND CIVILIANS

SHAPING POLITICAL DISCOURSE IN CAMEROON

TRANSLATORS, INTERPRETERS, MILITARY AND CIVILIANS

By

SARON MESSEMBE OBIA

Vij Books
New Delhi (India)

Published by

Vij Books
(An imprint of Vij Books India Pvt Ltd)

(Publishers, Distributors & Importers)
4836/24, Ansari Road
Delhi – 110 002
Phone: 91-11-43596460, M: 98110 94883
E-mail: contact@vijpublishing.com
Web : www.vijbooks.in

Dedicated to

Almighty God and Obia Sammy Sammy

"Of course, I want counsel. But it is even more important to have a good interpreter."

—*Hermann Göring, Oct. 29, 1945*

Contents

EXECUTIVE SUMMARY

The 2016 events in Cameroon attracted the attention of national and international media on the cultural sensitivity in the country. From the 'Major National Dialogue' to the creation of the 'National Commission for the Promotion of Bilingualism and Multiculturalism', and then a 'Special Status' attributed to the two English-speaking regions, is yet to heal the cancer.

From detention, interrogation, and court proceedings in the military tribunal, still reveal language challenges, particularly at the level of legal interpretation and terminology. As such, "Shaping Political Discourse in Cameroon: Translators, Interpreters, Military and Civilians" sheds light on the role of translators and interpreters in peacebuilding.

The book starts with a brief overview of Cameroon's complex and diverse linguistic history. It then delves into the need for training resource persons at the Ministry of Defense and Ministry of Justice, vis-à-vis the political tensions between English-speaking and French-speaking communities on cultural sensitivity in the country.

Language is a vector for civil-military relations, peacebuilding and sustainable development. The role of translators and interpreters in conflict areas is now, more than ever, essential for unity and sovereignty of the state. However, the military's definition of professionalism, which prioritizes military skills over linguistic skills, creates a negative framework for civilian linguists, who are often seen as deficient and untrustworthy. This can lead to misunderstandings and mistakes for both the interpreters and the military.

To overcome the clash of professionalism, it is necessary for the Advanced School of Translator and Interpreters (ASTI), University of Buea, to create a more inclusive environment for interpreters in the field of security. This would involve providing interpreters with the same level of training and respect as other military personnel. It would also include understanding the importance of cultural sensitivity in conflict-affected areas.

The book further discusses the role of interpreters in multinational military cooperation settings. Interpreters play a critical role in ensuring accurate and effective communication in these settings. They must have a deep understanding of both the languages involved and the cultural nuances of the different countries represented. However, interpreters face many challenges in these settings, including the need to be familiar with a wide range of languages and cultures, work in a fast-paced and stressful environment, and maintain confidentiality.

In order to overcome these challenges, interpreters need the right training and support, including language training, cultural training, and stress management training. It would also involve creating a supportive environment where interpreters feel valued and respected.

More so, the role of translators and interpreters in the criminal justice system. There is the right to a fair trial, regardless of their language abilities. This means that defendants who do not speak the language of the court must be provided with an interpreter. Interpreters face several challenges during criminal proceedings, such as the need to translate complex legal terms accurately, maintain neutrality, and work in a confidential setting. Adequate training and support, including legal training, neutrality training, and confidentiality and ethics are necessary for equity.

The major focus of this work is to understand the role of translators and interpreters in peacebuilding. Interpreters play a crucial role in ensuring accurate and effective communication in peacebuilding efforts. They can also help to promote understanding and cooperation between different groups, particularly in DDR centers. This would help mitigate errors and misunderstandings, which can undermine peacebuilding efforts. All these challenges appeal on the Ministry of Defense to invest in training and resources for interpreters working in conflict-affected areas to ensure peacebuilding and reconstruction.

ACKNOWLEDGEMENTS

First and foremost, I want to thank Dr. Moluh Seidou Mama, Dr. Liben Francois and Dr. Akoumou Catherine for the good conversations which inspired me to ask more questions, and challenge more ideas.

I am deeply grateful to Brig. Gen. Pradip K. Vij, Mr. Komlan Avoulete, and Mr. Charles Ebune, whose generous support made this work possible. I would also like to thank Rev. Dr. Ngalle S. Njie, Mr. Obia Ranndy, Mr. Obia Mboni Bryan, Mr. Obia Remmy B., Mr. Tamfuh Bright Njie, Miss Eyambe Mende Raisa, Mr. John Nambo Itoe, Mme Yong Renata Mbong and Mme Sylvie Eponle Usoh whose assistance and dedication was critical to the completion of this book.

I appreciate the continuous encouragement of Mme Sallygina Dieni Njibili, Miss Obia Brina Rose, Mr. Modika M. Daniel, Mme Modika Hilda Fembe, Mme Younti Kelly, Mr. Djapou Longa Franck Lyonnel, Mr. Fandjio M. Bernard, and Modika Efamba Rapheal.

Finally, to all students of the Advanced School for Translators and Interpreters (ASTI), University of Buea, staff of the Ministry of Defense and Cameroon International War College.

LIST OF ACRONYMS AND ABBREVIATIONS

AIIC	-	International Association of Conference Interpreters
ACFLS	-	The Army Culture and Foreign Language Strategy
ARI	-	Army Research Institute
ASTI	-	Advanced School of Translator and Interpreters
CAC	-	Combined Arms Center
CoEs	-	Centers of Excellence
CEFR	-	Common European Framework of Reference for Languages
CKC	-	Culture Knowledge Consortium
CFLAs	-	Culture and Foreign Language Advisors
DDR	-	Disarmament, Demobilization and Reintegration
DLIFLC	-	Defense Language Institute Foreign Language Center
DoD	-	Department of Defense
ENAM	-	The National School of Administration and Magistracy

ESIT	-	Interpretation and Translation at Hankuk University
FARP	-	Forward Air Refueling Point
GC	-	Geneva Convention
ICTY	-	International Criminal Tribunal for the Former Yugoslavia
ICRC	-	International Committee of the Red Cross
IMT	-	Initial Military Training
MEP	-	Mise En Place
MINDEF	-	Minister of Defense
PME	-	Professional Military Education
POIs	-	Programs of Instruction
QRF	-	Quick Reaction Force
STANAGs	-	Standardization Agreements
TCC	-	TRADOC Culture Center
TIC	-	Troops in Contact
TRADOC	-	Training and Doctrine Command
UN	-	United Nations
UNPROFOR	-	United Nations Protection Force
U.S	-	United States

CHAPTER ONE

INTRODUCTION

People define themselves in terms of ancestry, religion, language, history, values, customs, and institutions. They identify with cultural groups: tribes, ethnic groups, religious communities, nations, and, at the broadest level, civilizations. People use politics not just to advance their interests but also to define their identity.

— Samuel P. Huntington (The Clash of Civilizations and the Remaking of World Order)

Cameroon is a central African country of 475.000 km2, with a population of 19 million (2010 population census figures) inhabited by peoples of diverse ethnic groups with very few shared similarities, the Bantu in the Centre, South and East Regions, Semi-Bantu mainly in the West Region, and the Fulbe and Sudanese in the Adamawa, North and Far North Regions. Cameroon thus has a peculiar and complex linguistic setting. Bretton & Fothung (1991:20, in Anchimbe, 2006:44) reported two official languages (English and French), apart from Pidgin-English, "Camfranglais", and unspecified number of national languages[1] exist. However, the constitution only recognizes English and French as official languages.

---

1   Neba, W. T., & Amos, N. M. A. (2019). Ascertaining The Quality Of The Translated Version Of The New Cameroon Penal Code. Advances in Social Sciences Research Journal, 6(4)7-21.

The defeat of the Germans in World War II ushered in the French (the first entry) and the English (the second and educated English entry) through the Treaty of Versailles/Paris Peace Conference (1919). The end of World War I coincided with the death of German as an international lingua franca. In the new dispensation, French replaced German in East Cameroon annexed by France and English in Southern Cameroons annexed by the British[2]. While Southern Cameroons was administered from Nigeria where educated English had earlier on gained substantial influence through church missionary bodies and elementary and adult school programs, East Cameroon, for its part, was administered directly from France through the intermediary of resident French governors and administrators (Wanchia, 2012).

At the 'reunification' in 1961, both French and English were declared official languages of the *Federal Republic of Cameroon*, having thus been endowed with the unique originality of European-language bilingualism (Tchoungui, 1983:93). The two official languages were maintained even with the advent of the United Republic in 1972. Moreover, when the country became the Republic of Cameroon in 1984, the status remained unchanged.

Indeed, *Section 1.1.5 of the revised Constitution of 1996 (Law No. 96/06 of 18 January 1996)* states that *"The official languages of the Republic of Cameroon shall be English and French, both languages having the same status. The State shall guarantee the promotion of bilingualism throughout the country"*[3].

On account of the above, Cameroon is thus considered bilingual and bicultural, and has a bi-jural system. While common law, for instance, remained practised by the people

---

2 Ibid

3 https://www.cameroon-tribune.cm/article.html/29439/fr.html/bilingualism-
   promotion-inspiring-executive

formerly called Southern Cameroons, the civil law system, for its part, is practiced by the French-speaking former Republic of Cameroon. This remained so until internal wrangling sparked in the country, based on the status and form of the state.

More pointedly on November 26, 2016, Cameroon's bilingual, bicultural, and bi-jural character were undeniably questioned – the educational and legal sectors came under 'real attack' with far-reaching effects till date, as epitomized by the common law lawyers' strike that was followed by that of the education sector. Both English-speaking subsystems decried what they called 'infiltration and dilution' of these two sectors of their subsystem by Francophones.

The major point of contention in the legal sector was the transfer of francophone legal functionaries to common law jurisdictions, which undermines the language and practices used in the common law courts. Common law practitioners appealed on the abusive use of French language in common law courts – either the direct use of French to the English-speaking or the use of *poorly translated 'English versions' of texts.* The role of translators and interpreters has long been solicited in crisis and war zones. The demand for interpreters is high, as war remains pervasive in history and will likely continue in the future, so will the need for interpreters[4].

According to Baigorri (2003), there is always the necessity for interpreters when war, conflict or crisis emanate. During war, language and interpreters are exploited as weapons in order to control the media within the conflict. For this reason, war creates the sudden demand for interpreters, since language is

---

4   Read; Interpreters And Fixers In Conflict Zones: The Examples Of Iraq And Afghanistan by Pablo Márquez de la Plata Valverde. https://repositorio. comillas.edu/rest/bitstreams/209451/retrieve/

often a key aspect for civil-military relations, negotiations or dialogue and a path for national unity.

Rafael (2007) subscribes to Baigorri and other author's explanations, while highlighting that translation and other linguistical factors are essential in the warring context. Translation serves as a tool of surveillance in order to hear and understand what the enemy may say in a foreign language. Rafeal equally explains how great empires of history used translators and interpreters as an instrument of power in order to control colonial and conquered territories.

Inghilleri (2010), argues that the nature of war creates the classical friend/enemy division, the 'us' and 'them' distinction that is often caused by language as well as many other factors. In a warring context, language and culture play an enormous role that has to be fulfilled by interpreters. Ruiz Rosendo and Persaud (2016, 2018) added that conflict between groups of humans has always involved the role of the interpreter as a cultural and linguistical mediator, mostly through untrained interpreters, also known as fixers.

Bali and Moser-Mercer (2018) and Kahane (2007) adhere to the fact that war and conflict go far beyond cultural and linguistical boundaries, the reason for which interpreters are needed. Bali and Moser-Mercer (2018), Baker (2010) and Henchman (2016) further explain that, in conflict zones, interpreters play a significant part in intelligence activities throughout history, and even in the War Against Terror, like in the context of Cameroon (Boko-Haram) and Afghanistan.

With regards to the *Criminal Justice System*, when interpreters translate a witness's testimony during criminal proceedings, errors are not just possible, they are inherent to the process. Moreover, the occurrence of such errors is not merely a technical problem; such errors can infringe on the rights of defendants or even lead to verdicts based on faulty findings of fact. International criminal proceedings, which are necessarily multilinguistic, are both particularly susceptible to interpretation errors and sensitive to questions of procedural fairness[5].

In order to better understand the role of culture and intercultural communication in conflict or crisis zones it is necessary to provide a clear distinction between interpretation from translation. The word "translation" refers to "the transfer of thoughts and ideas from one language (the source language) into another (the target language)," in either written or oral form. Meanwhile, interpretation encompasses only oral communication and is defined as "situations in which one person speaks in the source language, an interpreter processes this input and produces output in the target language, and another person listens to the interpreted target language version of the original speaker's message."[6] Based on the situation in Cameroon, the term interpretation would be considered the more or less contemporaneous rendering of utterances into their equivalents in another language.

Interpreters in conflict zones - who offer their services in all stages of a conflict (Baigorri-Jalón 2011)- perform an essential role in a number of war-related scenarios: with intelligence-gathering activities[7] (Gómez-Amich 2016), on the frontline (Inghilleri 2009), during military interrogations (AlonsoAraguás 2015), in interactions with the local population (Hoedemaekers and Soeters 2009), and in advising missions with local armies (Hajjar 2016). In

---

5   Joshua Karton, Lost in Translation: International Criminal Tribunals and the Legal Implications of Interpreted Testimony, 41 Vanderbilt Law Review 1 (2021) Available at: https://scholarship.law.vanderbilt.edu/vjtl/vol41/iss1/1

6   Ibid

7   https://www.lourdesderioja.com/2018/06/05/the-interpreter-a-neutral-go-between/

such complex scenarios, a general taxonomy of the figure of interpreters in conflict zones seems to be complicated (Ruiz Rosendo and Barea Muñoz 2017), especially considering that there is a series of different interpreter profiles working in this kind of scenarios; military interpreters (military personnel who works as linguists), locally-recruited interpreters, humanitarian interpreters, UN language assistants, fixers, and staff interpreter (cf. Allen 2012; Ruiz Rosendo and Barea Muñoz 2017 for a more detailed classification of this figure).

The set of skills required for interpreters, however, tends to be quite complex and demanding. Nevertheless, some of these interpreters completely lack any sort of training in both interpreting skills as well as first aid and survival techniques. This is particularly true in the case of interpreters locally recruited, i.e., recruited in the country in conflict to which the international troops have been deployed.

This group of interpreters, which is the largest of all, refers to interpreters who are local citizens of the deployment country and are usually recruited because they speak the local languages/dialects (plus the troops' language) and because of their cultural, historical, and political knowledge. However, it is precisely this inside knowledge that accentuates their 'otherness' in the eyes of the international troops. In other words, it highlights the fact that they do not belong in the military context, but rather come from the same country and the same community as the enemy, therefore their in-group loyalties may be (considered) blurry. This situation is extremely delicate seeing that the military needs to hire a person from outside their institution, and paradoxically, give them access to sensitive information.

In this kind of scenarios, certain theoretical concepts such as trust, loyalty and neutrality take a completely different angle, as conflict zones involve several distinctive features capable of altering the invisibility and neutrality that, in theory, is expected of interpreters, regardless of the context in which they work. In these lines, for certain authors, neutrality in conflict zones is only an illusion, considering that interpreters are torn between allegiance to their native country and the neutrality that is expected from their profession (cf. Stahuljak 1999; Spahic 2014; Gómez-Amich 2017). As a matter of fact, the client (which in this case is the military) anticipates that loyalty, one of the main concerns in conflict zones[8], will primarily be, in the case of the interpreters, with their own country (cf. CALL 2004: 12) and, that in certain cases, these interpreters may even have hidden agendas resulting from their motivations, needs, ideology and patriotism. And, after careful consideration of such life-threatening scenarios, one cannot help but understand this lack of neutrality. How can your interpretation be neutral when the life of your countrymen, your community and even your own family is at stake? (cf. the case Hasan Nuhanović during the Srebrenica genocide).

Consequently, it appears that the role of interpreters in conflict zones tends to be perceived – by the military (Hajjar 2016) but also by the interpreters themselves (Gómez-Amich 2017) as that of an expert in the local culture(s) and language(s). Compared to other settings of interpretation, the interpreter in conflict zones seems to hold considerable power, performing as active agents working for the good of their country against a common enemy, even though, as a result of the pervasive sense of mistrust that characterizes interactions in conflict zones, they are to be potentially perceived by both sides as possible traitors.

---

8   Gómez-Amich, M. (2018) The heart of the conflict - Challenges, complexities, and paradoxes intrinsic to the role of interpreters in conflict zones

Types of Interpretation

The two types of interpretation commonly used in courtrooms are consecutive and simultaneous. In consecutive interpretation, the interpreter talks during pauses between the speaker's utterances. In simultaneous interpretation, the speaker's utterances are interpreted continuously, but inevitably with a slight lag. Consecutive interpretation is often preferred for opening and closing statements and when a judge questions the witness because it gives the interpreter more time to consider nuances and, therefore, is more accurate.

Conversely, interpretation for the defendant's benefit is always performed simultaneously, and examination of witnesses often involves a rapid back-and-forth and conversational flow that requires simultaneous interpretation. Simultaneous interpretation is usually performed with or without the aid of electronic equipment; the latter method is called chuchotage and involves the interpreter standing next to the witness and whispering into his or her ear.

In practice, nearly all interpretation in international criminal trials is simultaneous. For instance, suspected separatists of the Anglophone crisis who benefit from dual nationality. Interpreters tend to prefer to work simultaneously, so as to preserve the flow of the translated speech. More importantly, consecutive interpretation can be slow. At the 1945 San Francisco Conference at which the U.N. Charter was drafted, consecutive interpretation was used exclusively and "sessions were delayed interminably while translators slogged along well in the wake of the proceedings." International criminal trials often last years in any event, much longer than the San Francisco Conference and the utterances of the parties must be rendered at the same time into multiple languages.

Consequently, as a practical matter, international criminal courts must rely on simultaneous interpretation.

Drawing from Peter Uiberall's revelation, the chief interpreter for most of the first Nuremberg trial, found when he became chief that the interpreters had consistently been translating the German "*ja*" as "*yes.*" While "*ja*" can mean "*yes,*" it is most often used as a place-filler by German speakers in the way that English speakers might begin with "um" or "well" when responding to a question. Thus, when a German witness or defendant was asked a question about some possibly incriminating activity, association, or knowledge, his hesitation was interpreted as an unconditional admission. Then, "once that 'Yes' is in the transcript, the man is stuck."

Although interpreters describe themselves as "neutral mouthpieces," "invisible," or mere "bridge[s] of communication," they are actually none of these; the act of interpretation invariably alters the meaning of a speaker's utterances. As the prosecutor at the United Nations (U.N.) *International Criminal Tribunal for the Former Yugoslavia (ICTY)* acknowledged in that tribunal's first trial (*of Dusko Tadic*), "[a] great deal of accuracy is bound to be lost in the translation process. There is no statement taken during the course of the investigation that will be a verbatim report of what the witnesses say."[9]

Despite the high stakes involved, legal scholars and practitioners remain largely unaware of the way interpretation works and of the effect of interpretation on testimony. Instead, they view interpretation merely as a technical issue. For example, a lengthy article written in 2006 about a physician's testimony in international criminal trials never

---

9 ONGWEN TRIAL: Why The ICC Needs to Pay More Attention to Translation. https://masakeonline.wordpress.com/2015/01/28/ongwen-trial-icc-needs-to-move-fast-to-avoid-translation-becoming-its-new-achilles-heel/

mentions the issue of translation. The legal treatments of courtroom interpretation that do exist largely focus on the rights of minority or deaf defendants to have access to the services of an interpreter in criminal trials.

Historical background of Interpreters in Conflict

From the Peace of Westphalia to 1914

Nation-states and vernacular languages emerge the *European Peace of Westphalia (1648)*. These developments led governments to realize the importance of having their own representatives at foreign courts (Mattingly, 1937). French language replaced Latin as the lingua franca in diplomatic circles.

During this period, a new trend arose: interpreters played a much more visible role. The position of interpreters in armed conflicts also became more evident, as can be observed in the records of Napoleon's campaign to Egypt and Palestine (1798–1801), in which we find references to translators and interpreters who spoke French and Arabic. The Napoleonic wars is also found in records of the Russian campaign (Britten, 2000), where it is specifically mentioned that an interpreter was someone *"to whom all the details of the affair could be confided and who would repeat what he was told in the proper quarters"*[10] (Caulaincourt, 2011, p. 125).

During the same era, the position of dragoman emerged in the Ottoman court. These officials held a key role in the court, serving as language intermediaries between the Sultan and his bureaucracy (Lewis, 2005). The term comes from the Turkish *"trucheman"* and was anglicized to *"dragoman"* (plural: "dragomen"). Turkish dragomen wore a uniform, were paid relatively well, and were even allowed

---

10 https://rio.upo.es/xmlui/bitstream/handle/10433/3013/persaud-clementina-tesis16.pdf?sequence=1

to have assistants or student interpreters who, during their training, earned about one-quarter to one-half the salary of a fully-fledged dragoman. Other countries adopted the same pattern by establishing permanent foreign legations and representatives (Lee & Hocking, 2011).

Another crucial development during this period is that these professionals were trained for their duties. As early as 1806, *Prince Adam Czartoryski* urged the *Russian Emperor Alexander I* to establish a school of international relations and foreign service in order to suitably train future foreign representatives and intermediaries.

In 1714, the year after the *Utrecht Treaty* was signed, a new diplomatic practice was implemented; to wit, the "reservation" of the language to be used in the drafting of treaties[11]. Although French maintained its status as a lingua franca until the mid-20th century, English was becoming increasingly prominent during these years, due to the fact that from 1800 onwards foreign diplomats were received in English at St. James' Court. This practice was followed 60 years later by Lord Palmerston's statement that any government had the right to use their own language in foreign relations (Roland, 1999), which helped sow the seeds of change in the use of languages in the diplomatic world.

It is equally necessary to reveal that, from 1814-1914, treaties were drafted in French, although the conflict between English and French resurfaced as early as the *Second Hague Convention, in 1907*. After this date, speakers at international meetings used their own languages; such meetings, therefore, presumably required the participation of interpreters.

---

11 Ruiz Rosendo, L. & Persaud, C. (2016). Interpreting in conflict zones throughout history. Linguistica Antverpiensia, New Series: Themes in Translation Studies, 15, 1–35.

Pin-ling Chang's *"Wartime interpreting during the Sino-Dutch War (1661–1662)"* focuses on interpreting practices during the Sino-Dutch War (1661–1662) in 17th-century colonial Taiwan. He explored the role of the interpreter in war times as a subcategory of "conflict." The Sino-Dutch War was a protracted, multi-ethnic conflict between Europeans and Chinese, that required many written and oral interpreters mediated negotiations. Most of these interactions were carefully documented in the archives of the Dutch East India Company (*Vereenigde Oost-Indische Compagnie, VOC*).

Interpreters could, therefore, be seen as indispensable during conflicts or crisis. Pin-ling Chang regards interpreters' backgrounds, functions, status, issues of loyalty and trust and on interpreting and translation as a tool for manipulation and power struggle[12]. In the bid to develop a comprehensive understanding of the arts, the latter compares the interpreters and the interpreting practices during the Sino-Dutch War with our present experience, thus bringing to light some differences between the past and the present[13].

The Nuremberg trials

The Nuremberg trials, another major event held in the aftermath of a war, shaped the future of interpreting considerably. The trials began on 20th November 1945. In total, a series of 13 trials was held between 1945 and 1949 in Nuremberg, Germany. The first trial was conducted in four languages: *English, French, German and Russian*, the languages of the Allied Powers and Germany (Biddle, 1947;

---

12 Ruiz Rosendo, L. & Persaud, C. (2016). Interpreting in conflict zones throughout history. Linguistica Antverpiensia, New Series: Themes in Translation Studies, 15, 1–35.

13 The Palgrave Handbook of Languages and Conflict by Michael Kelly, Hilary Footitt, Myriam Salama-Carr Springer, 18 févr. 2019.

Roland, 1999)[14]. This is what is known as the Nuremberg Trial proper or Main Trial.

The other 12 trials, known as the Subsequent Proceedings, took place in German and English, as the tribunals for these trials were formed solely by American judges (Gaiba, 1998). The Nuremberg Trials were the result of a decision to prosecute *Axis leaders* taken in *Yalta by Roosevelt, Churchill and Stalin*. As early as 1943, the Allies had warned the Axis powers that any perpetrators would be made accountable for their crimes before a court of law. The Nuremberg Trials are considered the birthplace of modern conference interpreting.

The first time an official declaration was made with regard to the eventual prosecution of those responsible for perpetrating violence against European Jews and the civilian population in general was December 1942. The options for punishment of the perpetrators included a proposal to execute 50,000 to 100,000 German Staff Officers and the possible summary execution of the defendants. In the end, however, the American leaders' proposal of holding a criminal trial and treating the case as a German criminal plot prevailed, for a variety of reasons. The most important of these was that documentation and proof of the accusations during the course of the trial would avoid potential claims that the defendants had been judged and sentenced without evidence; this process also ensured the defendants' right to a fair trial.

Given the multilingual nature of the proceedings, language management issues were of vital importance from the outset. The linguistic diversity of those involved in the trial meant that interpreting would be required. Both whispered and consecutive interpreting had been used in multilingual forums in the past, but neither of these modes was considered

---

14 Ibid

ideal for use at Nuremberg—consecutive because it would unreasonably prolong the sessions and whispering because of the fact that the interpreter's voice would interfere with that of the speaker. Consecutive interpreting also required individuals who had already listened to the interpretation into their language to wait and listen to renditions in languages they did not understand. Consequently, the decision to use simultaneous interpreting was made (Baigorri, 2014a; Delisle & Woodsworth, 2012; Gaiba, 1998; Roland, 1999).

Texts discussing the Nuremberg Trials (Gaiba, 1998) name *Léon Dostert as the promoter of simultaneous interpreting at Nuremberg*. Convinced that if simultaneous interpreting was not used the trial would never end, he embarked on a mission to persuade the parties involved to use the new system. The decision to use simultaneous interpreting was finally made in October 1945 (Biddle, 1947; Gaiba, 1998). IBM provided the equipment free of charge and the necessary technical staff were trained to operate the equipment during the trials (Bowen & Bowen, 1985; Gaiba, 1998)[15].

Despite the linguistic diversity and its associated difficulties, the trial involved legal and procedural complications. One example of these hurdles is that the trial was an international one, thus bringing the laws of different nations, with their varied legal traditions and practices, into contact. Another complication was the fact that the tribunal's procedures had not yet been fully established. To resolve this issue, the rules of procedure enshrined in the *London Charter of the International Military Tribunal (issued on 8 August 1945)* were adopted. They included provisions such as requiring defendants to submit requests with enough time in advance for presentation of witnesses and documents related to their

---

15 Ruiz Rosendo, L. & Persaud, C. (2016). Interpreting in conflict zones throughout history. Linguistica Antverpiensia, New Series: Themes in Translation Studies, 15, 1–35.

cases; drafting a clear definition and categorization of crimes by combining Anglo-American and Continental law, in order to have a straightforward definition and distinction between crimes against peace, war crimes and crimes against humanity for the purposes of the trials and ensuring that both civilian staff and military officers could be charged with war crimes ("Nuremberg Trials", n.d.).

From Nuremberg to the 21st century

Drawing from a comprehensive study by Binhua Wang and Minhui Xu, entitled *"Interpreting conflicts, conflicts in interpreting – A micro-historical account of the interpreting activity in the Korean Armistice Negotiations"*[16], which examined one of the major historical events that shaped the geopolitical situation in East Asia after World War II. Other scholars have explored the *Korean Armistice Negotiations* that have dealt with international and national settings, the leading delegation members, and the major issues of the negotiations, such as the ceasefire arrangement, the demilitarized zone, and the repatriation of prisoners of war, and on the aftermath of the war (p. 187).

Kriesberg (1991) introduces the term *quasimediator*, that is, a person who may belong to one of the parties in conflict but is not officially appointed as a mediator. The idea of the translator as mediator is not new in translation studies. However, interpreters' mediating function is analyzed within the context of conflict mediation. Although the fundamental role of interpreters is to facilitate communication, the role of interpreters in conflict mediation and third-party intervention often goes beyond the usual role and skills needed by interpreters in other situations. Interpreters

---

16 Wang, Binhua & Xu, Minhui. (2016). Interpreting conflicts and conflicts in interpreting: A micro-historical account of the interpreting activity in the Korean Armistice Negotiations. Linguistica Antverpiensia New Series: Themes in Translation Studies. 15. 10.52034/lanstts.v0i15.402.

in conflict mediation need to be more sensitive to the background situation and to emotions, and they need to be able to sense perceptions and feelings. They also need to help the mediator create trust, open communication, and understand cultural differences and emotions.

In terms of geopolitics, geostrategy, inter-cultural communication and diplomacy, the Middle East region remains a relevant and formidable field of study of the most conflictive regions in the world. According to the *Global Peace Index (2018)*, countries like Afghanistan, Iraq, and the Syrian Arab Republic are among the top five most conflictive countries in the world, together with South Sudan and Somalia in Africa.

Scholars such as Ruiz Rosendo and Persaud (2016), Henchman (2016), Inghilleri (2010), Baker (2010), and Kahane (2007) claim that as long as there is conflict or war, there will be interpreters and translators filling the linguistic and cultural gaps, especially in international protracted wars like those currently taking place in Africa.

In order to understand the situation in the two Anglo-Saxon regions of Cameroon, it is necessary to review the dynamics of international security and terrorism, while interpreters are closely associated with the inter-cultural communication in the domain of Translation and Interpretation. Therefore, the need for a comprehensive national security strategy for peacebuilding in Cameroon.

In order to develop a comprehensive strategy, there is the need to understand the essential role of the interpreter in conflict settings. Thereby a review of the nature and working environment of this profession.

Security is cut across several issues, and to be suited to this discourse, the terminological difference that exists in this field of expertise must be clearly understood. Terms such as interpreter, fixer, stringer, linguist do not necessarily mean the same thing in different texts. The separation between 'national' and 'local' interpreters, which are also two entirely various categories of interpreters in order to avoid overlap and to be used in an interchangeable manner, would be erroneous.

Interpreter in Cameroon

An Interpreter is a national (Cameroonian citizen) or local individual who has received professional training as an interpreter; and is hired to carry out the function of interpreting for foreign correspondents, state institutions and private organizations and individuals. The latter must have undergone formal training in a professional institution or college and be certified as per the profession.

Local Interpreter: A local interpreter in the context of the crisis in Cameroon, is an individual who learned French and English by reading from books. He studied Interpreting at the Advanced School of Translators and Interpreters and became a certified interpreter. Following the military intervention in his community, he is hired to provide interpreting services.

A Fixer: A local individual in conflict zones like villages in the Northwest and Southwest Regions, who has not received professional training as an interpreter, and is hired to carry out the main function of interpreting for foreign correspondents or for the military. Additionally, they take on a wide range of infinite logistical functions that are not strictly defined. For example, a teacher who lives in Mamfe or Bamenda, who lost his job and has a mastery of the culture and communication skills, strategic areas hired by the state to provide interpreting services although he never received professional training of that kind.

Packer and M. Baker are the only authors that identify the fixer profile of usually being that of a young man who is an essential tool in helping foreign correspondents move around and also an essential tool against the local insurgency. Packer described them in the following way:

"They are generally young, cosmopolitan, quick-witted, stoical, tinged with idealism, implacable foes for their countries' extremists" (Packer, 2009).

Moreover, Palmer (2007) and Ruiz Rosendo and Persaud (2018) indicate that the majority of individuals who take the job of interpreting in conflict zones are fixers, not interpreters. Most of the so-called interpreters in conflict zones are locals who were hired because media personnel do not have enough cultural and linguistic knowledge of the conflict area. They reveal that fixers are hired due to their ability to adapt to different situations and military units, and also due to the fact that they can detect nuances in behavior that outsiders might not catch. While most fixers are ordinary local citizens, their profile is varied, ranging everywhere from university students to migrants and refugees. Fixers learn to perform the same job that professional interpreters perform without receiving professional training and advanced language training.

According to Palmer (2007), Miri (2014), Ruiz Rosendo and Persaud (2018), Inghilleri (2010), Takeda (2009), Hajjar (2016), Baker (2010) and Baigorri (2011) define an interpreter as an individual with professional training who carries out the function of interpreting in conflict zones. The professional training of the interpreter is precisely what differentiates him from a fixer. While a fixer can take on additional roles, such as acting as an informant, a mediator, a gatekeeper, a politically involved figure, a professional interpreter strictly acts out on his profession.

According to Palmer (2007), the role of the interpreter is exclusively the role of that of a technical relay, whose function is to guarantee the exchange of information from one language to another.

According to Ruiz Rosendo and Persaud (2018), the interpreter facilitates communication as he is able to speak both languages, interpret in both directions, and has the ability to cover a wide spectrum of topics that range from basic conversation to highly specialized themes. In other words, interpreters act as diplomats and mediators between different cultures and groups.

Meanwhile, Miri (2014) describes the interpreter as one who covers all the acts of communication that arise out of a conflict zone. She claims that interpreters play a vital role because they are the bridge between peoples. She also explains that the interpreter is necessary for any situation on the ground that requires communication, transmitting the concepts and ideas of the military towards the local population and vice-versa. But *Baigorri* (2003) is critical about the interpretation, and claims that an interpreter must fulfil a set of criteria in order to be considered one, such as knowing the languages that he is going to interpret and the culture in which the communication is taking place.

Furthermore, Palmer (2007) explains that in conflict zones, interpreters do not carry out word for word translation or interpreting, but rather a summary and synthesized version of what they hear. The reasons for this are: (A) that a lot of information they receive is simple straightforward information; (B) that a full translation would be lengthy and time-consuming, which could pose a danger or a hazard in a conflict scenario; (C) conversation in modern warfare conflicts involve languages like Arabic, Urdu, Pashtu, Dari etc., which are rich in cultural idioms, expressions, adornments, and detours, resulting in elaborate, even unclear messages.

Adding to what Palmer expressed in the previous paragraph, we found that Miri (2014) points out that there are instances in which the act of interpreting goes beyond the linguistic competence aspect. What is important is often not what is said, but what is expressed through culture, environment, religion, traditions etc. Interpreters often take on the role of interpreting cultural symbols, codes of social behavior, and often act as advisors if they perceive that it is better to act cautiously in a specific zone or moment. In this type of context, the interpreter assesses the immediate environment, knowing the language, the way of life of the locals, and the cultural and religious norms.

Inghilleri (2010) claims that unlike fixers, interpreters are not mediators, informants, intelligence gatherers, and gatekeepers. However, she stresses that interpreters may be asked occasionally to take part in interrogations, raids, patrols, and security operations, and translating war propaganda and intelligence data. To guarantee their own safety, they are often given body armor to wear, and they travel with the military units in armored vehicles.

Hajjar uses an allegory that says that the interpreter should be like a Swiss Army knife, possessing distinct cultural competences that range from diplomat, mediator, and innovator to subject matter expert, advisor, and combatant. Hajjar also points out that if the interpreter does his job very well, he will interpret not only what is being said, but also the subtle meanings and hidden messages in the conflict zone. Therefore, Hajjar stresses that the interpreter must possess skills that go beyond linguistical competence, his abilities must clearly go into the cross-cultural realm[17]. At the same time, Baker agrees with the previous authors and explains that interpreters were often required to go beyond their linguistic competences when it came to conflict scenarios.

Baigorri makes a similar claim by pointing out that interpreters sometimes take part in cultural brokering, as liaison officers, in diplomacy, in propaganda, in intelligence and counterintelligence activities, in combat behind enemy lines, and in interrogation of prisoners. These four authors claim that despite taking part in these activities, the interpreter does not step into fixer territory, he does not become a fixer or something else that is not an interpreter.

17 https://1library.co/document/yjewdxmq-interpreters-and-fixers-conflict-zones-iraq-and-afghanistan.html

Chapter Two

Theoretical Framework

It is always dangerous for soldiers, sailors, or airmen to play at politics. They enter a sphere in which the values are quite different from those to which they have hitherto been accustomed.

—Winston Churchill

The re-emergence of armed conflicts has increased visibility of translators and interpreters that accompanied this development, scholars both within and outside translation studies have begun to engage with various aspects of the role and positioning of translators and interpreters in war zones[1]. Media reports on contemporary conflicts and adopting a narrative perspective to make sense of how translators and interpreters are narrated by other participants in the war zone, including military personnel, war correspondents, mainstream media, alternative media, and local populations. However, their participation in elaborating the range of public narratives of the conflict, which is available to the public, usually influences the course of the war in ways that are subtle, often invisible, but nevertheless extremely significant.

Translators and interpreters working in war zones operate against a particular backdrop which inevitably has an impact

---

1   Mona Baker (2014) Interpreters and Translators in the War Zone Narrated and Narrators

22

on their role, their experience of the war, and how they are viewed by other parties. Two essential and interrelated elements of the public narratives that precede and accompany all wars constrain practically every form of interaction in this context, including the interaction between translators and their employers, compatriots, the media, government agents and other members of the societies in which they operate.

First, the issue of difference becomes central to each society's vision of the world and its relationship with others. Specifically, the 'other', the enemy, has to be narrated as radically different from ourselves if the violence of war is to be justified. The same stock political narrative is sold to publics on either side of every conflict, past and present: the enemy is evil, threatening, dangerously out of control and intransigent. It represents the opposite of everything we stand for: we are civilized, fair, level-headed, peace-loving, reasonable, and open to compromise. We value life and freedom, they are out to kill and enslave us (or our allies, or their own people). The potency of this storyline is such that despite its recurrent use to justify numerous wars, it continues to be easily and almost instantaneously activated as soon as an 'enemy' is identified by politicians and the media and war is declared. Where the translator or interpreter is then positioned, as one of us or potentially one of them, becomes extremely important and has concrete and often life-threatening consequences.

Second, a closely related element of this storyline is the assumption of homogeneity that heightens the perception of radical difference between us and them and leaves members of each society, including translators and interpreters, little or no room for maneuver – no room to negotiate a more tolerant, more accommodating relationship even with the odd member of the 'enemy' camp, and no 'in-between' space of the type that romantic theories of translation tend to assign them to. The enemy is typically narrated as consisting of a single, homogeneous group, as sheer evil, or *an undifferentiated menace*", as Packer (2007) puts it with reference to the way in which Iraqis working in the *Green Zone in Baghdad*, including interpreters and translators, are perceived by their American employers.

Germans in general were widely narrated as Nazis in the 1930s and 1940s; the word German itself became synonymous with Nazi. Similarly, Serbs were widely narrated as murderous during the recent Balkan wars, with Bosnians generally perceived as peaceful, helpless victims. Despite being portrayed as victims of an evil dictator in some narratives, with the rise in 'insurgency' since the invasion of their country in 2003, Iraqis have been consistently narrated as an undifferentiated source of threat, to the extent that, by 2006, the US military had replaced most Iraqi interpreters working in the *Green Zone with Jordanians*, and even invested in training citizens of the Republic of Georgia to take over in order to avoid relying on Iraqi interpreters – members of the them, enemy group (Packer 2007). As Packer reports, *"[t]he switch was deeply unpopular with the remaining Iraqis, who understood that it involved the fundamental issue of trust,"* particularly the ways in which interpreters and translators are narrated by other parties in the war zone, including the military.

Interpreters and Military Professionalism

Conflicts in the globalization era brought interpreting into close proximity with a military definition of professionalism which would have major consequences both for traditional representations of the neutrality of the interpreter[2] and for individual interpreters themselves caught up in the violence

2 Tesseur, W. and Footitt, H. (2019) Professionalisms at war? Interpreting in conflict and post-conflict situations. Journal of War & Culture Studies, 12 (3). pp. 268-284. ISSN 1752-6272 doi: https://doi.org/10.1080/17526272.2019.16 44415 Available at https://centaur.reading.ac.uk/85317/

of war. This clash of professionalisms was precipitated by major changes in Western military doctrine provoked by the events of 9/11 and their aftermath.

In the 1980s to the late 20th century, Western military narrative of war emphasizes the growing role of technology and imagines the future conflicts as battles which would be fought from an optical distance. By the late 1990s, however, with peacekeeping in the Balkans, and particularly with developments post 9/11, it was clear that troops now had to enter the countries concerned either on foot, occupying the territory, and staying there, in Iraq and Afghanistan, for example, for considerable periods. The role of technology became less relevant, while cultural awareness and an informed understanding of the local foreign culture became key tools of effective military intervention (Footitt, 2016: 211).

Language, to some extent, also became part of logistics and the kit of war, as Western militaries recognized that there would necessarily be on the ground encounters which would require oral communication and language understanding. The UK Military's view of linguistic communication was that language, just as much as culture, was a weapon to combat counterinsurgency:

UK military doctrine increasingly recognizes the importance of influence in achieving campaign objectives, reaching out to the hearts and minds of all those involved. This requires an understanding of culture and an ability to communicate our messages in a way that third parties understand, predominantly through language. Therefore, language cannot be neutral to those engaged with a crisis; if we choose to think otherwise, adversaries will exploit that choice and undermine our chances of success. (Lewis, 2012: 67)

NATO countries had for some time developed what the British called *'military linguists'* with proficiency levels agreed across NATO countries and codified in Standardization agreements (STANAGs), cross-referenced against the Common European Framework of Reference for Languages (CEFR)[3]. These covered the four language skills, but made no explicit reference to translation or interpreting, although interestingly enough, the British Army continued to use terms inherited from the UK Civil Service, alongside the STANAG levels, to describe language competence, with the stages 'interpreter', above 'colloquial speaker', and 'linguist' (Kelly & Baker, 2013: 32). For the army, however, language competences were not to be wholly a matter of language. They would be embedded in a notion of professionalism which gave the main priority to military rather than linguistic skills, languages were an 'add-on' to more important military competences, and it was recognized that if a soldier gained linguistic skills, this might actually inhibit his/her future career progression in the army (Footitt & Kelly, 2012b). This sense that military competences and objectives must always define professional linguistic conduct in the field served as a compelling negative framework for what the forces called 'civilian' linguists - locally recruited non-military personnel whom they were increasingly forced to employ in order to supplement the scarce numbers and sometimes inadequate linguistic levels of their own military linguists (Kelly & Baker, 2013: 70).

These civilian linguists were, by definition, professionally deficient in that they lacked the desired military professionalism, encapsulated in the term 'security clearance', that is to say unquestioned and proven loyalty to their

---

3   Tesseur, W. and Footitt, H. (2019) Professionalisms at war? Interpreting in conflict and post-conflict situations. Journal of War & Culture Studies, 12 (3). pp. 268-284. ISSN 1752-6272 doi: https://doi.org/10.1080/17526272.2019.16 44415 Available at https://centaur.reading.ac.uk/85317/

employer (the army), and insulation from the personal, social and emotional implications of the field of conflict (Kujamäki & Footitt, 2019: 122). American officers were recommended to employ local interpreters in Iraq; for instance, warned them to be mindful of the extent to which the civilian's personal views, ethnicity or gender could impact negatively on the success of the mission: *'Your translator might have an agenda, or his dialect or tribal affiliation might not be well received.... check in advance if female translator is OK'* (TRADOC, 2006).

Interpreters working with the army are usually confronted with a negative deficiency model, military professionalism narrative was always the baseline against which professional behavior and skills were being measured. The consequences of this model were to be considerable, both for the civilian linguists themselves, and ultimately for the military who employed them. At the outset of a deployment, the model allowed no space for the concept of what one might call alternative professionalisms, most notably of course that of interpreting. At first, in the hurried and chaotic first weeks of deployment, the pattern was generally ad hoc, with the army hiring civilians speedily on the spot. In this process, interpreters were defined as educated people who spoke English reasonably well. In Bosnia-Herzegovina, for example, those recruited by UNPROFOR (United Nations Protection Force) were students, sometimes high school students, teachers, engineers, who had generally received no training as interpreters. Bosnian interpreters interviewed as part of the Languages at War project for example related:

Some of them were studying English. The others didn't.... The others were kids like me. Like common kids, youngsters who were able to learn English in high school and pick it up to the level sufficient to get a job...

None of us at the time was a professional interpreter. Very few people actually had a degree in English Language[4]. No Never. We kind of learned along the way (Footitt & Kelly, 2012: 188, 184). The longer the Military stayed in an area, and the greater the linguistic demands made upon it, the more likely it became that these civilian language resources would be in some sense outsourced.

One US battalion in Bosnia-Herzegovina for example outsourced its interpreting via a civilian contractor who employed heritage language speakers (speakers of the foreign language who were US citizens). This introduced an intermediate tier between military linguists and civilian linguists, Category I: *since these people were American citizens, they had a security clearance, and they translated more classified information, and at meetings that were not, so to speak, available to local interpreters and local population'* (Kelly & Baker, 2013: 92). A professional hierarchy of interpreting was thus created in the field, with a scale of professionalism related to levels of security clearance rather than linguistic ability - military linguist, outsourced interpreter, and at the very bottom, the local civilian interpreter.

In these recent conflicts in Afghanistan and Cameroon, the relationship between civilian interpreters and military, set within these parameters, was marked by a tendency on the part of the military to deny subjectivity to the interpreters, since accepting such subjectivity could entail admitting the very qualities which officers had been warned against - personal agendas, ethnicities, gender considerations. Yet the failure to recognize and account for the fact that civilian interpreters were personally embedded in the fabric of their

---

4   Footitt, H., Kelly, M. (2012). Civilian Interpreting in Military Conflicts. In: Footitt, H., Kelly, M. (eds) Languages at War. Palgrave Studies in Languages at War. Palgrave Macmillan, London. https://doi. org/10.1057/9781137010278_11

society's war would prove a particularly life-threatening and toxic omission when troops left the zones concerned. At this point, the invisible left-behind interpreter emerged into the light of media scrutiny to the very considerable discomfort of the military themselves.

In the UK, for example, persistent and well-publicized press campaigns, particularly by the Times Defense correspondent, Deborah Haynes, confronted the UK Army with their failure of duty of care to employees which the logistics-based approach to language and interpreting had caused. Haynes' campaign calling on the UK Government to accept its responsibilities for interpreters employed in Iraq and Afghanistan, and offer them asylum or compensation was so effective in forcing the subject onto the political agenda and providing some support for local interpreters that the British press awarded her their *Rat up a Drainpipe award* for investigative journalism that had produced an important change in policy (Luft, 2008).

Interpreters and Professional Development

In contrast to the debates on interpreters involved in conflict situations, much less has been written on interpreters working in post-conflict settings. When international NGOs enter such spaces to set up development programs and support local communities and partners, they are confronted with linguistic barriers similar to those that military forces encounter when deploying troops abroad. The context, however, greatly differs: violent conflict and immediate danger have ceased, and emphasis in development projects is placed on collaboration and participation. Despite these differences, we argue here that as in conflict situations, the dominant profession of the development worker conditions the work and status of interpreters working in post-conflict settings, and this generally results in a low profile being attributed to languages and interpreting in development settings.

The empirical work we draw on to illustrate this point comprises thirty semi-structured interviews conducted in 2016 with NGO staff members, half working within the UK, and half outside, employed by four large UK-based development NGOs. The four NGOs, including *Christian Aid, Oxfam GB, Save the Children UK and Tearfund*, all have a considerable history of development activity since World War II, and are currently active in over forty countries. The staff interviewed held a range of posts, including managers, advisory officers, communications specialists, and translators. We here focus on what participants said about the role of translation and interpreting in their job.

What emerged from the data was the low level at which multilingualism and translation are institutionalized in NGOs? All but one NGO, namely Christian Aid, had an internal translation service in UK headquarters, yet these services tended to be based on the translation of written documents, and translation mainly occurred from English into a handful of strategic languages (usually French, Spanish, Arabic, in some cases also Portuguese).

These services did not respond to the need for interpreting between a wide variety of (local) languages and English or between other language pairs. Professional interpreters were occasionally hired to interpret at high-level meetings or conferences, involving diplomats, important donors, or politicians, but any interpreting needs outside such official or formal contexts would usually be handled by multilingual staff. NGOs do not usually hire professional interpreters because they 'have got people from pretty much every language in the world somewhere in the office,' although 'their key skills are not necessarily linguistics' (INT 33, translator, UK).

Modern Warfare: The Examples of Iraq and Afghanistan

The most recent and well-documented cases of interpreters in conflict zones are the ones in Iraq and Afghanistan. Both Palmer (2007), M. Baker (2010), and Takeda (2009) highlight the need for the use of interpreters that emerged with the Iraq war, the conflict in Afghanistan, 9/11, and the War on Terror. Interpreters have played the role of mediators in this context, being a crucial aspect for the success of military and intelligence operations.

Scholars equally explain that the Western powers have used both first-generation immigrants and local interpreters/fixers to cover the growing demand for languages such as *Arabic, Pashtu, Dari, Farsi, Kurdish* etc. Henchman (2016) explained that the need for the use of interpreters arose in Iraq and Afghanistan due to the nature of such wars, consisting of shadow warfare techniques, attrition warfare, guerrilla tactics etc. The language barrier and cultural differences meant a difficulty for the Western armies, and thus they had to hire interpreters who spoke Arabic, Dari, and Pashto.

Local interpreters being recruited and incorporated within the army units in order to communicate with the local population is usually crucial. According to Henchman (2016) and Packer (2009), local insurgency in both countries views the interpreters as a potential target, infidels, apostates, traitors, and spies for the West.

The Example of Iraq

Palmer (2007) reveals that the security conditions in Iraq heavily declined from 2003 onward, and that formerly secured areas for foreign media and their interpreters became too dangerous to access. Since then, more than half of the media personnel killed in Iraq were interpreters. Campbell (2011) and Kahane (2007) subscribes to Palmer's claim and reveal that Iraq was the country that had the highest interpreter casualties, alongside the military.

Inghilleri (2010) explained why mass casualties of interpreters in Iraq. He revealed that, on the battlefield, interpreters developed close bonds with the military units due to mutual dependence in such extreme conditions, which often led many of them to believe that they were somehow 'equal' to the military. In reality, they are not equals, local interpreters do not form part of the Western militaries and they are therefore not given sufficient protection in many cases.

The Example of Afghanistan

Miri has been the main author that wrote about the situation in Afghanistan. Miri (2014) argues that the insurgent menace in Afghanistan pose a massive threat to local interpreters, since they do not have the same protection that can be found in Western military bases. This is evident, with U.S withdrawal from Afghanistan, empowered Taliban.

Another aspect in conflict zones are cultural problems amongst the military and their interpreters. In Afghanistan, the beliefs of Islam demand that the interpreter and the foreigner respect a series of key factors when it comes to the act of communication. Islam is a religion with a lot of subtle codes of behavior that are hard to understand, marked by a strong tradition that dates centuries back. In this context, it is important for the Westerners to not meddle in sacred moments of Islamic prayer. Patrolling near a mosque during the hours of prayer can be interpreted in a hostile sense, Afghans appreciate when the foreign forces respect their holy hours. Miri further opines that interpreters have been key to unite the Western forces with the local population, since they have brought an influx of innovative ideas and points of view to the Afghan population.

Campbell (2011) subscribes to Miri's (2014) narrative and reveals that the menace on interpreters in Afghanistan is alarming. Both interpreters and international media are regularly victimized, when writing or interpreting against government corruption and organized crime. Campbell claims that in Afghanistan, the men behind corruption and the drug business are just as dangerous to interpreters as the Taliban's are. Moreover, security is another challenge, as Afghan interpreters often live with their families outside the military camps, in the outskirts of Kabul and other major cities, therefore being vulnerable to the Taliban.

In addition, Kahane (2007) and Witchel (2004) reveal that on different accounts interpreters and fixers are being kidnapped and killed by the Taliban or being detained, tortured, or charged under criminal offences by the country's authority

CHAPTER THREE

MILITARY NARRATIVE AND INTERPRETIVE THEORY OF TRANSLATION

A popular Government, without popular information or the means of acquiring it, is but a Prologue to a Farce or a Tragedy; or perhaps both. Knowledge will forever govern ignorance; And a people who mean to be their own Governors, must arm themselves with the power which knowledge gives.

JAMES MADISON to W. T. BARRY-August 4, 1822

The Interpretive Theory of Translation, also known as the "Theory of Sense" or the "Paris School," was developed in the 1980s by ESIT1 researchers and conference interpreters, Danica Seleskovitch and Marianne Lederer. Choi Jungwha, a professor at the Graduate School of Interpretation and Translation at Hankuk University (an ESIT alumni), outlines the Interpretive Theory as a concept built upon four pillars:

1) command of the native language,

2) command of the source language,

3) command of relevant world and background knowledge, and

4) command of interpreting methodology[1].

---

1 Conference Interpretation In The Military Environment Of Francophone West Africa by Julie A. House. https://www.ieee.es/en/Galerias/fichero/docs_

34

The first and second pillars refer to the command of one's native language in all of its nuances and the second language, the latter requiring a lifelong and open-ended learning process. Relevant world and background knowledge constitutes the third pillar which also involves a similar ongoing learning process. The fourth pillar focuses on the concept that the translation process requires an understanding of the sense of the original message and a formulation of the translation based on the synecdoche principle (Junghwa, 2003: 2). In essence, the mastery of both the native and the target language is required as a baseline or a prerequisite for the development and training of competent translators and interpreters. Acquisition of relevant background knowledge is a continuous process, and the accurate interpretation of the initial message requires the ability to understand the sense of that message and then reformulate that sense in a manner that is acceptable and understandable to the target audience.

Command of native and target languages

With focus on the first two "pillars" of the Theory of Sense, the mastery of both the native and the target languages is essential for an interpreter in order to develop the necessary skills to operate successfully in demanding multinational military settings. In most Sub Saharan countries military colleagues usually belief that most French native speakers are apt to serve as skilled French/English interpreter. This situation usually creates controversy as the English speaker is not usually acknowledged. For instance, military colleagues determine that they should, as a trained interpreter, should be replaced by an untrained native French speaker. However, the French speaker lack of training or experience as an interpreter, does not incapacitate his mastery of the military language. Some interpreters are usually confused

marco/2014/DIEEEM13-2014_Military_Environment_of_Francophone_West_Africa_Julie-House.pdf by the reversed pronunciation of the letters 'G' and 'J' when interpreting between French and English.

More so, understanding the value of native English skills and the necessity of a trained and experience interpreter is usually evident with his/her knowledge of conference discussions and technical terminology. Most at times an inexperienced interpreter possess extensive worldly knowledge and excellent communication skills which ultimately contributes to the success of a meeting.

Furthermore, the automatic choice of the "French native" English speaker over the non-native trained interpreter has had more negative consequences, leading to significant misunderstandings and frustration. For example, *a senior African officer was told by an inexperienced interpreter (native French) that his country would receive a multimillion-dollar aviation system when in fact the cooperation package in question was valued in thousands of dollars and referred to equipment to be employed by the country's Army on the ground. As the conversation continued, it became quite clear by the context of the conversation that the officers were indeed discussing ground-based equipment, but the interpreter continued to refer to an aviation system. Although the interpreter soon understood his error, he was unwilling to admit his original mistake. Ultimately, the senior diplomat present clarified the interpreter's error in order to avoid future misunderstandings.*

It was revealed that the interpreter had been hired based on the fact that he was a native French speaker, a person who resided in a Francophone country until age 12 and furthered his education in the United States[2]. The defense contractor, hiring the individual, based employment decisions on the individual's résumé but did not have an interpreter accreditation process in place. In such situations, the

---

2   Ibid

interpreter's shortcomings are unfortunately identified as the result of misunderstandings provoked by a lack of training or poor mastery of one of the two (or both languages) involved. In this particular instance, the senior diplomat rectified the situation before the miscommunication could lead to more significant misunderstandings.

The Defense Industry understands the necessity of reliable and loyal interpreters because Cameroon has more than 210 local dialects and there is need for cultural liaisons. As such, "the success of the Cameroon and allied mission, as well as the lives of soldiers" depend on capable interpretation.

Command of relevant world and background knowledge

The third pillar of the Interpretive Theory emphasizes the persistent requirement for acquisition of knowledge, to include worldly, general knowledge and more precise knowledge that pertains to the specific situation of communication. In the case of multinational military cooperation settings in Francophone West Africa, knowledge acquisition must consider worldly knowledge as it affects the overall geopolitical situation on the continent and in the region while emphasizing the multifaceted cultural aspects pertaining to this unique environment.

In this respect, the interpreter's must concord that relevant knowledge acquisition is a process, most important lessons will be learned on the ground, but thorough prior preparation and an understanding of the cultural elements involved will serve to enhance the quality of interpretation and improve overall communication.

The language barrier and the attitude on an individual limited by linguistic capacity and a lack of background knowledge has led many people to believe that the recruits are usually incompetent ingrates, whereas an interpreter's obligation is to promote improve communication by providing feedback to the supported organization.

Socio-Cultural Aspects of West African Military Cooperation Environments

The previous example represents a multitude of social settings characterized by cultures (both military and non-military) that, depending on the quality and fidelity of interpretation, may potentially collide or coalesce. At a minimum, the interpreter must strive to reformulate the message in a manner that respects the originator's intention, with the associated cultural nuances, thereby fostering mutual understanding.

In a military cooperation environment like West Africa, successful communication must be based on the premise of cultural understanding and respect among peoples, among military organizations and even within a single country's own military. According to Marianne Lederer, translation difficulties are most often triggered by problems confronted at the intercultural level. Often, one finds that the particular notions of one culture do not have corresponding lexical equivalents in another (the target culture). And even if one does manage to adequately express these notions, there is no guarantee that the reader (or listener) will understand these notions. In essence, finding the right word in the target language will not suffice. The interpreter must know how to express the implicit messages contained in the original text (Lederer, 2006: 102).

In the military cooperation environment of Francophone West Africa, the potential for translation difficulties increases exponentially due to the variety of cultures represented. It is impossible to express the multitude of cultural variations found across this region of Africa.

Military interpreters are confronted not only with the challenges presented by the obvious cultural differences (linguistic, social, and ethnic), but also with the distinct inter and intra-military cultures present in this environment also increases the complexity of their task. The military interpreter will be collaborating with African military officers, non-commissioned officers and soldiers whose linguistic upbringing and military training reflect formal French schooling and institutions, but whose professional training increasingly reflects training and interaction with new international partners.

Military culture and protocol

Throughout West Africa, one finds traditional, centralized organizational structures consistent with traditional French influence, but several nations are now pursuing modernized, professional militaries in collaboration with not only France, but also the United States, Russia, Israel, China, Japan, and several other international partners. To cite an example, Malian, Niger, Burkina Faso and Cameroon reflected the training of certain officers in Russia and Israel. Their concept, knowledge, tactics, and operational capacity were different than that of their counterparts whose training was limited to French and local programs.

East Africa or West Africa, the militaries of Francophone countries adhere to specific protocols and respect certain unspoken rules which differ from the Russian and American military service member. Most of these countries' militaries operate under more formal hierarchies with a more pronounced separation between the officer and enlisted ranks. In the U.S. Army, for example, enlisted service members receive in-depth technical and professional training early on in their careers. As a soldier approaches the ranks of the non-commissioned officer (NCO), he is expected to accept more responsibility, and training becomes increasingly more focused on the development and perfection of leadership skills. On the contrary, the West African soldier will rarely be assigned significant responsibilities and once promoted to the NCO ranks, any leadership expectations will be limited due to the traditionally centralized military structure common to most West African militaries. With the emergence of coups in West Africa, most countries are trained by Russia Wagner, which fight alongside national military detachment to maintain the sovereignty of the state.

An added advantage to interpreters born in Anglophone Cameroon and raised in Francophone Cameroon, is their fast apprehension of the cultural nuances common to several West African countries. However, the costume is another psychological element for interpreters in military meetings. If the organizers observe the interpreters' rank is low, certain officers will refuse or ignore his interpreted messages due to the rank of the officer. But if the latter adopt civilian clothes, senior officers suddenly turn to respect the latter for his exceptional skills and will always be solicited for senior-level and ministerial discussions pertaining to the exercise.

U.S. military protocol, by contrast, is often perceived by African counterparts as too informal. Our "mission comes first" mentality and achievement-oriented energy, generally considered proactive and positive within the U.S. environment, often lead us to commence meetings without respecting daily protocols that serve to form the foundation of relationships across African partnerships. Experiences on the continent have taught us to respect the extra five minutes of courteous salutations and polite conversation that so often precede meetings with African counterparts. Even the simple morning handshake that is expected when operating in company with French military partners is occasionally misunderstood. The American racing by with a well-intentioned "Good morning!" may be perceived as inconsiderate for ignoring an outstretched hand. The interpreter plays a key role in understanding and respecting such sociological and cultural differences, not only within and between the various militaries, but also between the various ethnicities and nonmilitary social groups represented during military engagements conducted in Francophone West Africa.

West African culture and the impact of oral tradition

Military cultural differences are based on the fact that the military interpreter is more likely to initially comprehend and relate to cultural differences and similarities on a military level. As relationships develop and friendships are forged, the interpreter will gain valuable insights into the ancestral, social, cultural, or national experiences unique to the environment. For example, in spite of colonial influences, the populations of this region have managed to successfully preserve and respect certain oral traditions that have been passed down from one generation to the next for hundreds of years. Once initiated, the outsider begins to notice and understand certain unspoken and spoken intentions present in the West African military dialog. Among so many examples of these cultural "lessons learned," one particular episode stands out.

A few years ago, I was caught off guard by the comments of a Burkinabé Gendarme lieutenant. We had just been introduced and continued to converse as we entered a conference hall to attend a ministerial-level meeting related to security cooperation initiatives in northern Burkina Faso. As we greeted the other military officers assembled for the meeting, the lieutenant then turned to the Minister of Transportation and proudly stated, "Bonjour, Esclave!" to which the minister pleasantly replied, "Hello, Master."

The interpreter is a peacebuilder. Drawing from the above exchange, the interpreter had to choose correct words for the conversation. Though the young lieutenant had just called the minister a "slave", he further made use of oral tradition referred to by many in this part of the world as "parenté à plaisanterie", a sort of regulated social code founded on joking relationships established between specific ethnicities or groups of people, a code that not only allows interlocutors to insult one another but actually encourages such behavior. The Burkinabé tradition was a product of the regulated and long-established "slave/master" relationship between the Samo and Moose ethnic groups of the region. In as much as, the minister clearly outranked the lieutenant, but in this case, oral tradition trumped formal state protocol rules. This tradition plays a fundamental role in the mitigation of social conflicts and serves to foster cohesion.

Socio-cultural knowledge acquisition and preparation

Comprehension of the innumerable social and cultural nuances unique to the milieu requires continuous general research, detailed preparation prior to each specific military engagement activity, and experience on the ground. While certain knowledge can only be gained through direct experience, the interpreter can facilitate and improve knowledge acquisition by consulting human sources or experts in a given field and by preparing personal glossaries that are tailored to the subject matter and terminology pertaining to the specific event (Gile, 2009: 151).

Interpreters and translators in the military milieu need to collaborate with others in order to understand and have a clear sense of integrated words. For example, translating French ISAF-adopted acronym "TIC" (troops in contact) as a part of their routine operational vocabulary. Hence the challenge for the interpreter or translator that will rely on a

French language source without the knowledge that certain terms are actually Anglicized.

Moreover, the French military's regular adoption of English acronyms, such as FARP (Forward Air Refueling Point) and QRF (Quick Reaction Force). However, acronyms like "MEP" stands for Mise En Place, this appeals for a comprehensive understanding for military terms or acronyms before translating or interpretation. Both AFRICOM interpreters and French LNOs work in bilingual environments daily, therefore ongoing collaboration is helpful to both parties[3]. This relationship, however, should be expanded to include all Francophone assets. I have often collaborated with French officers that confirm the translation of a phrase or acronym used regularly by the French Army only to be corrected later by an African officer confirming that his country's army uses a different term.

The real challenge presents itself when the French and African officer are in the same room disputing the correct use of a certain term, as Anglophone officials are standing by asking for a concise interpretation of the conversation. In this case, who is right? Often, both are right. Although both armies speak the same language (French), the terminology and argot for each have evolved as a function of the diverging experiences of each, hence the aforementioned ISAF-adopted French use of the U.S. acronym "TIC" to describe troop contact with the enemy.

These are just a few examples provided to underscore the importance of focusing knowledge acquisition on the social and cultural diversity characteristic of the military environment of Francophone West Africa. The U.S. military's fondness for "roadmaps," is adequate enough to provide an

---

3   https://www.ieee.es/Galerias/fichero/docs_marco/2014/DIEEEM13-2014_
Military_Environment_of_Francophone_West_Africa_Julie-House.pdf

interpreter's attention to an apt metaphor that serves as a model to facilitate application of the Interpretive Theory in the culturally complex environment in question.

Daniel Gile (ESIT Paris) refers to a cultural "roadmap" in which each language and its associated culture can be linked to a set of available road signs. When producing a source speech, the "Senders" use the signs available in the source language and places them along the roads of a particular route. The translators use signs available in the target language and place them along the same general route. The main objective of the translator (or interpreter) is to provide the "Receiver," or end user, a concise message by the Sender. As far as possible, the translators must try to place their signs in a configuration that is consistent with the Senders' use of their own signs. When reading a translation, Receivers have time to stop and look at the signs along the way, perhaps note a particular selection or arrangement of signs, approve, or disapprove.

On the other hand, listeners, when listening to a speech (to include the interpreter's speech), travel at high speeds and have less time to contemplate the individual signs. For translators, it is therefore important to be able to select and place target-language signs carefully so as to lead Receivers to the destination along a route closely resembling that depicted by the Sender, whereas for interpreters, "it is more important to be able to drive rapidly to their destination, following speakers at an imposed speed" (Gile, 2009: 73-74).

Operating in Francophone West Africa, military interpreters have the advantage of an innate understanding of at least one set of these "cultural road signs," specifically those indicators that refer to sociolinguistic and cultural aspects of the general military environment. This understanding also serves as point of common ground between U.S. interpreters and their multinational counterparts.

In essence, such international military camaraderie forms a foundation upon which linguistic and cultural collaboration can be developed thereby enhancing the quality of interpretation and ultimately, the effectiveness of communication. Development of a dedicated cadre of trained professional military conference for interpreters would offer this and many other advantages.

Development of a military conference interpreter program

The military interpreter often is the first to initiate communication on the ground, and as the initial "voice," this person enjoys the first opportunity to establish report between partner nations involved in the particular event.

In some respects, the interpreter and the foreign service member are speaking the same military language, a particular jargon that an inexperienced civilian interpreter would not automatically understand. In this regard, the military interpreter is one step ahead given past knowledge acquisition and regular access to new, evolving information that is relevant to the military setting in question. Some information is automatically acquired through the interpreter's daily exposure to military events and doctrine. Due to his integration in the military organization, he understands the Department of Defense's strategic objectives and relevant mission requirements that are unique to his own service branch and to his particular command.

In addition, the military interpreter must be well-versed in service-specific and joint military jargon and acronyms. Equally, the latter is subject to military ethics and discipline and is held accountable for performance and actions.

The military interpreter's support for the decision-making process

The aforementioned information advantages, combined with thorough preparation and ongoing knowledge acquisition, enable the military interpreter to better support the leadership's decision-making processes. For example, understanding the Commander's Intent or the Commander's Critical Information Requirements related to a particular military event helps the interpreter to better express the intentions of the interlocutors involved. For example, an assigned interpreter for members of National Security Council during meeting at the presidency in Cameroon. The meeting which focused on the potential for military cooperation initiatives with civilians ahead of back to school in the two English speaking regions in Cameroon.

Military cooperation is usually sealed based on facts and reasonable proof of attacks on the host country or one soliciting assistance. The choice of words used by an interpreter files the quest for the country. For example, the president's interpreter translates the words "brigand" and "bandit" as "terrorist" to a U.S audience. It may sound erroneous, but this proof the interpreter is aware of certain guidelines and restrictions that would govern the United States' ability to provide military training and equipment. Specifically, Section 1206 of the National Defense Authorization Act grants the Department of Defense certain authorities to provide such training and equipment to foreign militaries. 1206 programs, however, are specifically limited to programs directly linked to counterterrorism efforts.

The translation of bandit as terrorist is to lull the U.S. DoD to be favorable to the terms of security cooperation initiatives. This adheres to the fact that, military interpreters, with the requisite language skills, a high level of professional interpreter training and experience, and the analytical capacity to process and communicate relevant situational knowledge, would offer military leadership a key strategic advantage.

Review of U.S. department of defense training initiatives

In 2010, the U.S. Department of Defense (DoD) published its Defense Strategic Plan for Language Skills, Regional Expertise, and Cultural Capabilities, 2011-2016 (Hagan, 2020)[4]. The plan revealed the DoD's commitment to further enhance language and cultural skills of its service members while improving regional expertise and understanding.

In terms of linguistic capabilities and cultural awareness, the DoD recognizes the need for vast improvement across the board. The strategic plan emphasizes language acquisition and cultural immersion by promoting new methods, including training collaboration with international counterparts. The DoD currently invests a significant amount of time and money to provide valuable language training to personnel. For example, the Cameroon government should ensure personnel of MINDEF and ENAM acquire language, translation and interpretation skills at the Advanced School for Translators and Interpreters, courses offered in English, French, Arabic, Spanish and Chinese, among others. This will help certain soldiers or civilians recruited in the ministry of defense to qualify the military linguist as a professional translator or interpreter. Language programs focus on the mastery of the foreign language, but translation is generally limited to what would be deemed school translation.

The Cameroon government should create Defense Language Institutes like in the U.S, which provides translation and interpretation skill development in eight-week courses for native and heritage speaking soldiers as part of their

---

4   https://apps.dtic.mil/sti/trecms/pdf/AD1114546.pdf

Advanced Individual Training[5] in order to adapt in crisis areas.

The re-affirmation of security cooperation with Asian and other European countries will require the state to expand the program to the Pacific and European partner countries. With this, interpreter/translator training programs will expand to include new language pairs. Perhaps the Army will also consider the reciprocal value of its professional interpreters possessing native English-speaking capabilities.

Professional training for military conference interpreters

Increasingly, international military cooperation in West Africa involves direct involvement with not only senior military officials, but also with senior diplomats and representatives from strategic international organizations such as the United Nations, the African Union, the European Union, and NATO[6]. The military interpreter operating in this complex international arena must be capable of performing up to the professional interpretation standards to which these international organizations are accustomed.

As Daniel Gile (2006: 9) asserts, *"Top level interpreters are required to be able to make speeches at a language quality level expected from the personalities they interpret, be they diplomats, scientists, politicians, artists, intellectuals, and appropriate for the relevant circumstances: press conferences, political speeches, scientific presentations, intellectual discussions, etc".*

The military interpreter must be up to the task, whether that means rendering an interpreted message appropriate for the partner nation's senior government officials or communicating with school children during a civil military

---

5   https://www.ieee.es/Galerias/fichero/docs_marco/2014/DIEEEM13-2014_Military_Environment_of_Francophone_West_Africa_Julie-House.pdf

6   https://www.hrw.org/news/2005/05/24/darfur-help-african-union-boost-troops-now

coordination activity. A tailored conference interpreter training program based on the Interpretive Theory of translation and developed in accordance with International Association of Conference Interpreters (AIIC) recommended standards will enable military interpreters to the requisite level of competence to successfully manage the challenges presented in the multinational cooperation environment.

Echoing the first two pillars of the Interpretive Theory of Translation, AIIC underscores the mastery of working languages and excellent command of the native language as a prerequisite for basic conference interpreter capability. Reading Danica Seleskovitch attests, « Pour l'interprète, la connaissance de plusieurs langues n'est pas un but en soi; c'est un préalable indispensable pour que l'interprétation telle que nous avons tenté de la définir puisse s'effectuer » (Seleskovitch, 1984 : 126). In effect, for the interpreter, knowledge of several languages is not a goal in and of itself but rather an indispensable prerequisite for the conduct of effective interpretation.

Initially, the training program would adhere to certain best practices for interpreter training programs as identified by AIIC:

- A language aptitude test would be required for both the native and the working language(s) prior to commencement of the course. Access to the course would be based on demonstrated mastery of the languages concerned.
- Courses would be taught by qualified conference interpreters.
- The curriculum would include instruction in both consecutive and simultaneous
- interpretation.

> ➤ The course duration would be 3 semesters long.

During the first two semesters of the course, interpreters would learn the necessary techniques for effective interpretation (for example, note-taking for consecutive interpretation) while focusing heavily on knowledge acquisition skills and interpretation methodology consistent with the Theory of Sense. The curriculum management of interpretation difficulties that may present themselves in real-world situations of communication: jokes, technical difficulties, ethical challenges, conflict, or arguments, etc.

The third and final semester would be dedicated to knowledge acquisition in a practical environment. One of the three primary goals set forth in the DoD Strategic plan goal is to strengthen language skills, regional expertise, and cultural capabilities of military personnel in order to increase interoperability and to build partner capacity. To achieve this goal, the plan sets forth the value of capitalizing on the language skills, regional expertise and cultural capabilities of international partners and allies (DoD Strategic Language Plan, 2011-2016). This third semester would involve an extensive in-country training program, similar to the familiarization training conducted by U.S. Foreign Area Officers. For example, the interpreter trainee would spend the semester in a Francophone West African country, working in the military environment and collaborating with military interpreter counterparts.

The purpose of this final semester would be to offer the military interpreter similarly rewarding experiences that would ultimately serve to improve interpreter proficiency and increase cultural awareness while building relationships and reinforcing international partnerships.

In the West African security environment, in particular, the successful interpreter must comprehend the basic foundations of communication in the regions, to include the indelible impact of oral tradition, Indigenous languages, colonial history and current geopolitical developments[7].

Further, the interpreter must have a clear understanding of the military cultures involved in each situation of communication. In this regard, military interpreters have a distinctive advantage over their civilian counterparts. The establishment and employment of a cadre of professional American military conference interpreters, selected based on command of their working languages and then trained in an intensive professional conference interpreter program, would serve to reinforce relationships among our African partners and ultimately, to improve military cooperation across the region.

---

7   Ibid

CHAPTER FOUR

COURT INTERPRETER IN CRISIS ZONES

The role of translators and interpreters' cuts across several professions; the criminal justice system (lawyers, magistrates, court clerks) are equally involved. Inghilleri (2008, 2009) and Maier (2007) have examined the role of translators and interpreters in judicial milieu, specifically those who are captured by the intelligence institutions or the military and accused of terrorism or insurgency. Inghilleri (2008, 2009) and Rafael (2007,2010, 2009) have several studies or on media reporting on the treatment and fate of interpreters in contemporary wars, mostly in Iraq and Afghanistan.

According to Inghilleri (2009) a wide range of published accounts of the Iraq war which occasionally make mention of translators and interpreters, such as Thomas E. Ricks' Fiasco: The American Military Adventure in Iraq (2006) and Tony Lagouranis' Fear Up Harsh: An Army Interrogator's Dark Journey through Iraq (2007). However, the best study that examines the use of translators in intelligence gathering in the context of war is Footitt (2009, in press), who focuses on intelligence activities based at Bletchley Park (UK) during World War II, and specifically on the involvement of linguists in translating material from decrypted coded messages and captured enemy documents.

By its very nature, and given official secrets acts and other restrictions on accessing such data during and for some time after a war has ended, research on the role of translators in intelligence gathering activities is inevitably scarce and subject to the same limitations as other research based on the examination of war archives. There is no doubt, however, that translators and interpreters continue to play an important though often undocumented role in intelligence gathering activities. Packer (2007) mentions several examples in the context of the recent invasion and ongoing occupation of Iraq. Journalists are better equipped to investigate the actual war context, and in more recent years, media reports – often quite detailed – of firsthand, witness accounts and interviews with translators and interpreters working on the battleground have been easier to find. These reports have appeared in a wide range of print and online media, both mainstream and alternative. English publications include *The New York Times, The New Yorker, The Washington Post, Christian Science Monitor, Los Angeles Times, The Guardian, The Independent and Harper's Magazine,* among others, and similar reporting has featured in print and online media in other languages.

In recent conflicts, particularly Iraq and Afghanistan, journalists have begun to engage with the issue of language mediation and to register more awareness of the translator as a distinct participant in the events being narrated. This is a largely untapped source that scholars ought to make much better use of in future. Maier (2007) takes a very cursory glance at media reports. While Inghilleri (2008, 2009) draws on media reports occasionally, but not systematically.

The duty of the Court Interpreter is to serve as a conduit between non-English speakers and English-speaking officials in legal forums. As they convert one language to another, interpreters play a critical role in the administration of justice and make it possible to ensure the rights of due process and participation in the court system for all those involved. The goal of a court interpreter is to enable the judge and jury to react in the same manner to a non-English-speaking witness as they do with one who speaks English. Also, the limited – or non-English-speaking defendant should be enabled to hear everything that an English speaker has the privilege to hear.

The proper role of the interpreter is to place the non-English speaker, as closely as linguistically possible, in the same situation as an English speaker in a legal setting. In doing so the interpreter does not give any advantage or disadvantage to the non-English speaking witness or defendant. The goal of a court interpreter is to produce a legal equivalent, a linguistically true and legally appropriate interpretation.

Court interpretation for foreign language speaking and deaf or hearing-impaired individuals is a highly specialized form of interpreting that cannot be effectively performed without commensurate specialized training and skills[1]. Being bilingual, even fluently so, is insufficient qualification for court interpreting. Interpreters must be able to interpret with exactitude while accurately reflecting a speaker's nuances and level of formality. The interpreter must interpret the original source material without editing, summarizing, deleting, or adding; while conserving the language level, style, tone, and intent of the speaker. The interpreter must render what may be termed the "legal equivalent" of the source message.

The nuisance in the criminal justice system in Cameroon

A judicial officer must appoint a qualified interpreter for persons handicapped in communication to prevent injustice and to assist them in defending themselves. Court administrators and judges should be aware that many people who need an interpreter will not request one because they do not realize that interpreters are available or because

---

1   https://docplayer.net/18335682-3-role-of-the-court-interpreter.html

they do not recognize the level of English proficiency or communication skills needed to understand the court proceeding. Therefore, when it appears that an individual has any difficulty communicating, the court administrator or judge should err on the side of providing an interpreter to ensure full access to the courts.

Criminal Proceedings

Using U.S as example, Minnesota has declared a state policy that it will make qualified interpreters available in criminal and related proceedings to persons who are "handicapped in communication" to ensure the protection of their constitutional rights. For these individuals, a presiding official must appoint a qualified interpreter to prevent injustice and to assist them in defending themselves whenever they:

(1) cannot fully understand the charges made against them;

(2) cannot understand a proceeding which may subject them to confinement, criminal sanction, or forfeiture of property; or

(3) are incapable of assisting in their defence.

A "qualified interpreter" is one who is readily able to communicate with the person in need, interpret the proceedings for the person and accurately repeat and interpret the person's statements to the official before whom the proceeding takes place.

A presiding judge must appoint a qualified interpreter for the defendant in all proceedings, including, but not limited to, a coroner's inquest, grand jury proceedings, depositions, arraignment, plea hearings, every stage of trial including *voir dire* and return of the verdict, sentencing, and probation hearings. Because of the threat of confinement, the presiding judge must also appoint a qualified interpreter for mental health commitment proceedings.

In addition, a qualified interpreter must be appointed for a witness in need of interpreter services who appears at any of these proceedings. If the court has difficulty locating a qualified interpreter, the proceeding should be continued. If good faith efforts are being made to secure an interpreter, the defendant's right to a speedy trial is not necessarily violated by a reasonable delay.

In all criminal proceedings where an interpreter is used, the best practice is to make an audio recording (or videotape when a sign language interpreter is being used) of the proceedings to ensure an avenue for challenging interpreter accuracy in the event that the fairness of the trial is questioned.

The Case of Nkongo Felix Agbor-Balla and Others Cameroon[2]

Cameroon is a bi-lingual and bi-jural country as a consequence of its colonial experience. In reality, the Anglophone system is confined to two regions out of ten in the Northwest and Southwest of Cameroon. The emerging point of contention by public and professionals in these regions, in particular, barristers, teachers, and journalists that the Anglophone system and English language is receding due to the increasing appointment of public officials in local administration that speak only French and are not familiar with the Anglophone legal or educational systems.

The Yaoundé Military Tribunal has jurisdiction over the first-instance trial proceedings. The court has special jurisdiction to hear some of the charges pursuant to Law No. 2014/28 of

---

2   Jodie Blackstock (2017) Trial Observation Report Nkongo Felix Agbor-Balla and Others Cameroon. Bar Human Rights Committee

23rd December 2014 on the Suppression of Acts of Terrorism in Cameroon.

The Court has national jurisdiction, which can be exercised where there is concern about a case being tried in the local vicinity. The Court sits in the military barracks in the center of Yaoundé, capital city of Cameroon. The bench comprises an army colonel magistrate, who is the President of the tribunal and two lay assessors from the navy and air force.

The proceedings originally indicted three accused persons, Mancho Bibixy, also known as BBC; Fontem Aforteka'a Neba (who I will refer to as Fontem Neba) and Nkongho Félix Agbor-Balla (who I will refer to as Felix Agbor). The indictment, which is in French, appears to record that the:

"Yaoundé Military Tribunal has jurisdiction for the purposes of prosecution over the acts during November and December 2016, since according to the report of the Central Service for *Judicial* Research and its accompanying documents, there is sufficient indication that[3]: Mancho Bibixy together and in concert [presumably with others and in particular with the two other accused, though this is not specified] did:

> 1) commit an act likely to cause death, endanger physical integrity, cause bodily injury or material damage, destroy natural resources, the environment or cultural heritage with intent to:
>
>> a) Intimidate the public, provoke a situation of terror, or face the victim, the government and/or a national or international organization to carry out *or* refrain from carrying out an act, adopt or renounce a particular *position*;

---

3   Ibid

2) Take part in hostilities against the Republic of Cameroon;

3) Begin to violate the integrity of the state by claiming the partition of Cameroon through the creation of the State of Ambazonia;

4) Attempt by violence to modify the constitutional laws, in particular by claiming federalism;

5) Provoke the gathering of insurgents and destroyed public and private buildings;

6) Defame the President of the Republic and members of the Government;

7) By violence prevent the enforcement of laws regulations and legitimate orders of the public authorities;

8) Fail to produce his national identity card.

Fontem Neba and Felix Agbor were arrested on 17th January 2017 in Buea in the Southwest region of Cameroon where they lived and taken to Yaoundé. Mancho Bibixy was arrested in the early hours of 19th January in Bamenda in the Northwest region of Cameroon. The indictment charged Mr. Bibixy, Mr. Neba and Mr. Agbor on the 20th of January 2017, and asked for the Yaoundé Military Court to take jurisdiction and pass judgment and to remand the three in pre-trial detention.

On 1st February 2017, the case was due to be brought to court but for reasons unknown it was adjourned until 13th February. On 13th February, the charges were read out to the accused in French. An interpreter was present to interpret into English but there were concerns that the interpretation was inaccurate. The defense barristers made representations that the problem was that despite being arrested in an English-speaking region the court was constituted in the

Francophone region with French speaking judges and it was unconstitutional to be charged in French when the accused are English speaking. There was some suggestion from one of the defense barristers that the interpreter was reading from the wrong charge sheet, rather than interpreting what they heard.

The President of the Tribunal suggested that an adjournment would be necessary to obtain another interpreter. Felix Agbor asked that they continue but requested a more competent interpreter in future. The note further records that the State Prosecutor argued that the accused are perfectly bi-lingual, and it would be bad faith if they alleged that they could not understand the proceedings.

Furthermore, the country is bilingual and both languages can be used interchangeably. As such they decided to issue the charge sheet in French. He stated that both English and French are used in the Northwest and Southwest regions and so either of the two national languages could be used.

The charges were then put to the accused persons in English. All three pleaded not guilty. The court then sought to confirm whether counsel represented the accused. Former Battonier (President of the Cameroon Bar Association) Ben Muna confirmed that a team of lawyers would be representing the accused out of the over 100 who were present in the courtroom. The note then goes on to detail that he and other presenting barristers made submissions about the political nature of the trial and compared it to the previous occasion in 1991 when another lawyer had been put on trial for sedition, Yondo Black, who had been critical of the one party system under President Biya and attempting to establish a multiparty system with others, nine of whom were also on trial. They were convicted of sedition and given sentences from two to five years, though some were acquitted. On this occasion the demand had been for federalism and the second and third accused had been in negotiations with the Government to broker reforms at the point when their organization was banned, and they were arrested.

The defense argued that the accused persons were only exercising their rights as Cameroonians, as a journalist, a teacher, and a lawyer to exercise their freedom of thought, conscience, and speech. They also underlined the political realities that were taking place in the Northwest and Southwest regions, with the internet suspended and children not going to school. They called for dialogue to continue.

The barristers asked the State Prosecutor for a list of the State's witnesses and the evidence against the accused so that the case could proceed. The State Prosecutor argued that the accused were not arrested in the exercise of their professional duties. Further, that the Criminal Procedure Code enables secret police investigations and that only the Legal Department (the prosecution office) has access to the case file, which it will produce at the hearing as evidence. However, their list of witnesses was not complete, and they were still undertaking investigations. He asserted that the Court was competent under article 12 of the Law on the Suppression of Terrorism.

The defence challenged this, referring to the Criminal Procedure Code in that once a person is brought before the court, the correct procedure should be followed, and further investigations are not possible. They observed that this was the second hearing in the case, the accused were held in detention and the prosecutors should be ready to proceed on the charges that they have brought. They asserted that if the witnesses were not already known, the defense will view any that are subsequently brought to court with suspicion. The prosecutor replied that many witnesses are reluctant and in hiding.

Civil Parties

Three lawyers who sat in the rows in front of the public seating then stood up, walked to the bench, and handed up documents of appearance for civil parties. The defense team objected and asked for whom they were appearing. Counsel submitted that to appear in opposition to another lawyer, who is one of the accused, there must be permission pursuant to Law No. 90/059 of 1980, which requires in articles 39 and 47 proof that they are advocates and that the appearance is in accordance with the laws of the Bar, which requires permission of the Bar President to appear against another lawyer.

Prosecuting Counsel made submissions that they generally agreed with the defense interpretation of the criminal procedure code that it was not appropriate to adjourn. Because there was no interpretation, the accused looked vacant, confused, and bored at what was happening. At this point they were beginning to struggle withstanding in what was an extremely hot room.

The defense team then asked if their application for release from detention had been considered. They sought a decision from the application filed on 23rd March. No copy of the application was in the court papers so a defense copy was taken to photocopy. This took around 15 minutes to organize. I was later informed that this was the second copy of the application to go missing as an earlier attempt to file the application had met with the same problem.

At 2pm Karim Khan QC, of the Bar of England and Wales, who had an ad hoc appearance granted in the case, appealed on behalf of Mr. Neba and Mr. Agbor[4]. This was all interpreted for the President, but he had to regularly repeat his submissions for the interpreter to understand. He explained that an application for release was filed on 23rd March 2017 that had been before the court for more than a month. He argued that the only appropriate course was release and set out lengthy and respectful submissions to the Court as to why this was appropriate. He set out the educational and professional attainments of the accused, which made them, in his submission, extraordinary and for whom the nation should be proud rather than accuse as terrorists. He highlighted that they had been in custody for three months already and explained the hardship to their families.

He highlighted that the Constitution of Cameroon and the Penal Code required precedence to be given to international treaties signed by Cameroon over domestic laws and argued the application of the UNDHR, ICCPR and African Charter and other ratified international instruments applied directly to the case.

Interpretation and Translation

"[I]t is a prerequisite of the right to a fair trial, for a person to be tried in a language he understands, otherwise the right to defence is clearly hampered. A person put in such a situation cannot adequately prepare his defense, since he would not understand what he is being accused of, nor would he apprehend the legal arguments mounted against him."

The interpretation or translation provided shall be adequate to permit the accused to understand the proceedings and for the judicial body to understand the testimony of the accused or defense witnesses.

---

4   Ibid

Sections 354 and 355 provide for interpretation in court, to be appointed by the Presiding Magistrate and where an interpreter does not give a true and faithful interpretation, either the parties to the proceedings or the court of its own motion may replace the interpreter. The President of the Tribunal, when I had the opportunity to speak with her, said that the interpreter in this case was appointed at the request of the accused rather than the Tribunal, although it can be the case that the Tribunal also needs one. Cases are often heard with an interpreter because of the many Indigenous languages spoken in Cameroon, and in particular the Boko Haram cases before the Military Tribunal.

In Mgwanga Gunme the African Commission recognized that Cameroon is a bilingual country. Its institutions including the judiciary can use either French or English: "However, since not all the citizens are fluent in both languages, it is the State's duty to make sure that, when a trial is conducted in a language that the accused does not speak, he/she is provided with the assistance of an interpreter. Failing to do that amounts to a violation of the right to a fair trial."

In this case, an interpreter was present, but having interpreted the first few announcements of the President, did nothing further until the application for release from detention made in English by Karim Khan QC, which she interpreted into French for the benefit of the Tribunal bench. Despite the suggestion that interpreters were extensively used, it seemed few of the court professionals were used to using an interpreter effectively. None, other than Karim Khan QC, broke down their submissions and waited for the interpretation to be given, which made it hard for the interpreter to know when to intervene. Initially she stood, waiting to provide interpretation but when no opportunity came to do so, she sat down and did nothing.

There was a marked contrast in their concentration on the proceedings between the submissions being made in French, where they were restless and uncomfortable standing in the heat of the room, and those in English, where they were attentive and interested. Although Cameroon is a bilingual country, as the report of the Special Rapporteur on Minorities found, most people speak French. It was also clear that the interpreter struggled to understand the legal language in English being used during the bail application and interpreted this with difficulty, regularly requiring each submission to be repeated.

An interpreter who is unable to interpret provides no assistance to the accused. The trial was of Anglophone people. It should have been held in English rather than French. To have no interpretation into English was a clear violation of the rights of the accused to understand the case against them.

Interpreters in International Humanitarian Law

International humanitarian law recognizes the usefulness of interpreters as persons required for the proper functioning of a number of legal safeguards, as per the Third and Fourth 1949 Geneva Conventions. Specifically, Arts. 96 and 105 of the Third Geneva Convention (GC) outline the right of prisoners of war who are involved in disciplinary or criminal proceedings held by the Detaining Power to avail themselves of the services of an interpreter during the course of such proceedings. Similar Arts. 72 and 123 as per the Fourth GC, focuses on the protection of civilians detained by another State, in situations of military occupation or internment, who have criminal or disciplinary procedures brought against them. These provisions thus seek to ensure the right to a fair trial for persons protected by IHL.

Furthermore, the crucial importance of this right has been recognized by the ICRC's study on customary IHL which, under Rule 100, specifies the customary nature, applicable in both international and non-international armed conflicts, of the duty to provide an interpreter to persons who may be involved in criminal or disciplinary procedures, and in doing so also refers to similar provisions which have developed over time within human rights treaties regarding proceedings against foreign nationals.

It is also worth pointing out that such interpretation services, in view of their clear importance in ensuring the overriding right to defense, are given a special qualification. As per article 105 of the third GC: «the right of an accused prisoner of war to have the services of a competent interpreter "if he deems necessary" automatically results from the rights of defense if the language currently used in the detaining country is unfamiliar or unknown to the prisoner of war. In this connection, it should be noted that it is for the prisoner himself to judge whether he needs an interpreter. The word "competent" denotes an interpreter who not only knows the two necessary languages – that of the prisoner of war and that of the detaining country – but also is familiar with legal terminology and accustomed to acting as an interpreter during judicial proceedings. This interpreter must be supplied by the detaining power; if the prisoner of war prefers to have the services of one of his fellow-prisoners with the necessary qualifications, he may do so, provided that the person appointed also enjoys the confidence of the court»[5].

More so, this right can only be said to be fulfilled if the person entrusted with providing the service has the necessary qualifications to do so. These qualifications also include familiarity with legal terminology and being accustomed to acting as an interpreter in legal proceedings. An interpreter

---

5   Geneva Convention (III) on Prisoners of War, 1949 https://ihl-databases.icrc. org/en/ihl-treaties/gciii-1949/article-105/commentary/1960?activeTab=und efined%22%20%5Cl%20%22_Toc42465449%22%20%5Ct%20%22_blank

so defined must be provided by the detaining power or, alternatively, a fellow prisoner may be chosen, for obvious reasons of confidence. However, even in the latter instance, the condition that the interpreter be "competent" must in any case be met, which confirms that the standard established by the Convention is particularly high.

Finally, the provisions of the Geneva Conventions also envisage the use of interpreters to assist a protecting power. Article 126 of the third GC and article 143 of the fourth GC provide that members of delegations of the protecting power may avail themselves of interpreters in their monitoring activities, which may for example include visits to prisoners of war camps or internment facilities. In some cases, interpreters can be isolated in order to ensure direct contact, without any mediation interposed between the members of the international delegation and the protected individuals, so as to avoid any fear on the part of the interviewees that the confidential nature of the information they provide might be breached. Although the detaining powers have the obligation to provide such interpreters, particularly for members of the international delegation or individuals provided by the ICRC, in order to prevent interpreters from being seen as potential informers of the detaining power.

Thus, by scrutinizing these specific provisions, we have already been able to bring to light two aspects which are apparently central to the debate on the role of interpreters in armed conflicts. One is the need to ensure the technical reliability of the services provided by interpreters, in view of the requirement that the persons used should have qualified linguistic skills and, in particular, a knowledge of legal terminology. The other is the need embodied in these provisions to address the possibility that interpreters may act in an equivocal manner, such as to favor one of the parties to a conflict, and the further possibility that they may make use of their position as linguistic mediators for ulterior purposes, such as reporting any negative opinions expressed by prisoners and internees regarding the detaining power since these are the only provisions under IHL that directly refer to the services of interpreters in conflict situations, we must now seek to outline their legal status: (a) in the conduct of hostilities; and (b) with regard to their situation if captured.

The Legal Status of Interpreters during Hostilities

Concerning the conduct of hostilities, the main point to be clarified is the legal status of persons acting as interpreters, both when they are acting on behalf of one of the parties to the conflict and when they are assisting agencies or individuals which are not parties to the conflict, such as international organizations, journalists or NGOs. It is necessary to provide a clear distinction as to whether interpreters can be considered as combatants or civilians. It is also necessary to distinguish between international and non-international armed conflicts.

In international armed conflicts interpreters are usually excluded from the category of combatants, apart from the marginal case in which they are members of the armed forces of a state, the so-called military interpreters. This is rarely not the case as several armed forces have been enrolling members specialized in this activity for centuries. For instance, in 1803, in view of the planned invasion of England, Napoleon created the military corps of "Guides interpreters", which constituted commissioned officers and soldiers responsible for translation services operating among the so-called *"Army of England"*. A similar military unit, is the *Corps of interpreters* of the African army, was established in 1830 to facilitate operations in Algeria, and included former Mamelouks of Napoleon's imperial Guard.

Contemporary era security departments rely on military interpreters for their activities. Equally, in non-international armed conflicts, in order to qualify certain members of non-state organised armed groups as distinct from the category of civilians and therefore as targets of attack on an ongoing basis it must be ascertained that the individual shall have a "continuous combat function." It would however be hard to define the activity of interpreters as such, in view of their non-involvement in a proper combat function. Therefore, interpreters, even when acting on behalf of a party to the conflict, are usually considered civilians and thus protected against direct attacks.

The only possibility may arise in cases in which an interpreter carries out activities which could be characterized as a "direct participation in hostilities", as he would lose his immunity from direct attack. Considering the ICRC guidelines on this subject, which identifies criteria to classify a number of activities under this role, particularly for mediation and to enable linguistic communication, as direct participation in hostilities.

On the contrary, a different case could be made with regard to activities more closely related to tactical intelligence functions, such as the translation of encrypted or enciphered messages or military communications issued by the opposing side. In this latter case the activity involved is more specifically military in nature and is such as to confer a clear benefit to the party availing itself of the translation services in view of subsequent tactical operations. As such, this activity would probably entail the loss of immunity for civilians engaging in it, although we are obviously outside the normal realm of activities undertaken by interpreters.

In relation to cases in which interpreters provide their services to other actors present in the area of conflict, such as representatives of international organizations, NGOs or media professionals, the correct way to qualify such persons would be as civilians and there would seem to be no way in which they might be deprived of their right to be protected from direct attack. Obviously, when interpreters are present in the area of conflict, particularly in the exercise of their functions on behalf of a party to the conflict, there is a possibility that they will be indirect victims of warfare. However, certain situations can make the latter a legitimate military target, in as many as possible civilian casualties must obviously comply with the usual legal limit of proportionality.

The Legal Status of Interpreters in Case of Capture

IHL provisions as they govern the case of interpreters captured during armed conflicts. The legal status will first examine the case of interpreters who were performing their activity on behalf of a state which was a party to hostilities when captured. This category of interpreters' provision is outlined in the third GC, under article 4.A. (4), as «persons who accompany the armed forces». This specific provision attributes the qualification of prisoner of war to individuals who, while being civilians in relation to the conduct of hostilities, may find themselves captured, particularly in the event of ground operations, because the supporting activity they have been providing caused them to operate in proximity to enemy lines. Since the early codifications of IHL, it has been considered possible to attribute the prisoner of war status to these contractors, under certain conditions, as their position when captured had given rise to difficulties during past conflicts. Individuals serving as interpreters on behalf of state armed forces could be included within this special category, also because of the non-exhaustive nature of the list of activities referred to in this provision.

The only condition required in order to claim said special status would be for the individual to be acting with the authorization of the armed force which the latter is providing a service to; this required link is also attested to by the delivery of a special identity card. Apart from this specific instance, interpreters would still be considered as belonging to the civilian population. Thus, once captured, interpreters shall be entitled to the guarantees enshrined in the fourth GC, supplemented where appropriate by the provisions of the first additional protocol, as long as they can be qualified as "protected persons."

Therefore, in order to benefit from the status of "protected person" one must not be a citizen of the capturing state, as provided under *article 4* of the fourth GC, which defines the scope of application ratione personae of the treaty. This may have major consequences in the case of a state which is a party to a conflict making use of local interpreters, i.e., citizens of the state against which military operations are being conducted. in this case such individuals, once captured, would no longer fall under the protective provisions of the fourth GC, but would at least benefit from the protections granted in *ARTICLE 75 AP I*.

In the case of non-international armed conflicts there is, of course, no notion of prisoners of war. However, even in such a case, if captured by one of the parties, interpreters acting on behalf of one of the parties to the conflict, i.e. the government armed forces or the organised non-state armed groups, or even on behalf of other persons operating in the area, such as journalists, governmental or non-governmental organizations, etc., shall benefit from the safeguards established in the relevant provisions relating to individuals who are not taking an active part in hostilities. These guarantees are set out in the common article 3 of the 1949 GCs, in the second additional protocol, where relevant, and in the many rules of customary law which have been developed on this matter.

Interpreters involved in post-conflict situations

In recent times most interpreters are involved in a post-conflict situation. This would usually involve international organizations, or ad hoc coalitions of states, operating in international missions entrusted with peacekeeping and reconstruction tasks. In such cases, other international law provisions can be of use to define the legal status of interpreters. Particularly relevant could be the provisions provided by the status of force agreements (SOFA), i.e., treaties defining the legal status of personnel employed to assist an international mission.

In these conventions, a number of provisions can be significant for interpreters, especially local ones, as they can be equated with a category which is commonly regulated in these instruments, namely «locally recruited personnel». For example, the case for the United Nations' Model SOFA. In this document, after recalling in Paragraph 22 that the United Nations «may recruit locally such personnel as it requires», a number of rules are set out, clarifying privileges to such staff, usually identified with a special identification document provided by the UN authorities.

In particular, paragraph 28 of the UN–Model SOFA extends to locally recruited staff a series of privileges included in *section 18 letters a, b, c of the 1946 Convention on Privileges and Immunities of the United Nations*. Some of these privileges are explicitly re-affirmed in para. 46 of the SOFA, where it is established that members of the UN operation «including locally recruited personnel shall be immune from legal process in respect of words spoken or written and all acts performed by them in their official capacity». This privilege remains valid beyond the end of the mission. Moreover, pursuant to para. 48, immunity from local jurisdiction is also extended to civil actions in regard to disputes concerning the performance of official duties.

Similar provisions are also to be found in SOFAS covering other international operations outside the UN system. However, these provisions do not rule out possible prosecution being brought by states other than the one where the interpreter is operating. Depending on national laws, there may be a number of instances in which it is possible for personnel serving in these international contingents to be subject to a state's jurisdiction. One possibility would involve the application of the passive personality principle. A second possibility would be to base the prosecution on specific provisions extending the jurisdiction of a state, in relation to military offences, to civilian personnel working for its own armed forces, independently of their nationality.

The possible obligation interpreters may incur to give evidence before

According to fellows of the International Criminal Courts challenges might arise for interpreters operating in conflict zones. It is clear that, in view of the sensitive nature of the work performed by interpreters, they may be witness to particularly significant events or statements, which might result in their receiving subpoenas from international criminal tribunals to give evidence on activities connected with the performance of their duties. However, some International Criminal Tribunals, in particular the International Criminal Tribunal for the former Yugoslavia (ICTY) and the International Criminal Tribunal for Rwanda (ICTR), are endowed with the power to compel testimony from individuals considered to be useful for the investigation by issuing subpoenas for the compulsory appearance of witnesses which, if not complied with, could entail criminal prosecution being brought against recalcitrant.

The possibility of being summoned to testify clearly raises problems of professional ethics for interpreters, who are usually required to act on a confidential basis, and the issue of balancing the requirement of justice with the need to guarantee the safety of interpreters present in conflict areas, which would be further jeopardized if the parties to the conflict considered these persons as potentially inconvenient witnesses to the offences being committed. Precisely in order to address the various issues involved, international tribunals have in their practice developed a series of special privileges for certain professional categories, which may be exempted from the obligation to give evidence in view of the overriding importance of the functions they perform, compared with the need to obtain information which may be of use in the cases tried.

ICTY is a reference to such cases, as the tribunal has tackled the issue extensively, focusing on international presence on the ground, such as ICRC delegates and journalists, it is also possible to derive guidance from its rulings in defining the position of interpreters regarding these cases. The ruling made by the ICTY in the ***Delalic case***, in which the defense had advanced a request for a subpoena to be issued to an interpreter working at the tribunal in relation to some divergences emphasized by the defense during an interrogation. The trial Chamber rejected the request to compel the interpreter to testify. The tribunal evoked both the position of impartiality and the duty of confidentiality of interpreters and the necessity «to insulate the interpreter or other functionaries of the international tribunal from constant apprehension of the possibility of being personally involved in the arena of the conflict, on either side, in respect of matters arising from the discharge of their duties». This event was significant, as it underlines the need to avoid exposing interpreters to undue pressure in the performance of their official duties, in view of the importance of ensuring that they can properly undertake the tasks assigned to them.

However, the Delalic case relates explicitly to the work of an interpreter who was a member of staff of the ICTY; the situation might be construed differently in the case of interpreters working in a conflict area who are employed not by similar international institutions but by other organizations or individuals, such as journalists. The latter case is particularly significant, since the legal principles developed by the ICTY concerning the possibility of compelling journalists to give evidence were discussed as part of the **Randal case**, the events of which primarily involved a local interpreter hired by this journalist.

Randal, who at the time was a correspondent for the Washington post, had interviewed Radoslav Brdjanin, a member of the Republika Srpska administration, through a local interpreter, since the journalist did not speak Serbo-Croatian. the published interview quoted Brdjanin as using expressions denoting feelings of open hostility towards Bosnian Muslims.

In 2001, during the proceedings held against Brdjanin, the prosecutor sought to have the article admitted as evidence but the defense invoked its right to cross-examine the journalist to assess the truthfulness of the text. The tribunal responded to the request by asking Randal to confirm the accuracy of the sentences attributed to Brdjanin and to this end issued a subpoena against him.

Randal, however, challenged this procedure, alleging that journalists were exonerated from the obligation to give evidence and invoking his inability to provide any value judgement on the accuracy of the statements attributed to the defendant as he had had to rely on the services of a local interpreter. The trial Chamber refused to recognize the privilege invoked, whereas the Appeals Chamber partly accepted the journalist's position.

Even if it did not recognize an unconditional exemption for journalists from the requirement to give evidence, the appeals Chamber outlined a number of abstract judicial criteria to be used in deciding whether journalists working in war zones should be compelled to give evidence. The appeals Chamber ruled that the criteria had not been met in this case, particularly in view of the fact that his testimony would not have been of «direct and important value to determining a core issue in the case», in view of his inability to provide useful information on the accuracy of the translation.

The uncertainty surrounding these issues is confirmed by the ***Rules of Procedure and Evidence of the International Criminal Court***. In this case ***Rule no. 73 (2)***, concerns communications made "in the context of a class of professional or other confidential relationship" which shall be considered privileged in nature and thus not subject to the obligations of testimony or disclosure.

Rule 73 (2) outlines a set of criteria designed to define whether said privilege may be considered to apply to these kinds of professional relations, emphasizing in particular the confidential nature of the relationship; it also provides, in paragraph 3, some examples of these possible situations, even though they are characterized as non-exclusive and, more importantly, subject to the satisfaction of the aforementioned requirements. A specific mention is made of activities carried out by delegates of the ICRC, as well as the professional relationship between: patients and physicians; psychiatrists or psychologists; counsel and defendants and the activities of religious clergy, whereas no agreement was reached on the issue of journalists present in a conflict area, leaving the problem to be settled on a case by case basis.

However, neither during the negotiations nor at any later stage does any specific attention appear to have been dedicated to the case of interpreters involved in such situations, even if, for instance, they are usually obliged to perform their activities on a confidential basis. There are certain privileged people identified by ICRC in relation to the service of interpreters.

Notwithstanding it is essential to note that, when interpreters are providing official services related to the activity carried out by categories of professions covered by such a privilege, should also see this benefit extended to them, in view of the instrumental incorporation of the functions performed by linguistic mediators within the sphere of interest of the activity for which this benefit is recognized.

Chapter Five

The Role of Translator and Interpreters in Peacebuilding

In the current security environment, states are faced with an increasing array of regional and international challenges, risks, and threats (security, societal, ethnic, economic, and political). The military, the professional entity tasked with preserving peace and preparing for war to maintain it, remains also, the main organization responsible for engaging in these complex non-military security contexts, prepared for countering the global menace. Thus, it is estimated that skills and knowledge officers will need, today and in the near future, have changed due to specific circumstances altered by the increasing number of humanitarian and peacekeeping missions.

To respond, timely and effectively, modern military forces must develop and maintain a high degree of adaptability: officers must learn and embody enduring principles of combat and warfare, based on effective command and leadership. On the other hand, their teaching and training should, for that purpose, adapt to meet contemporary challenges, demands, gaps and opportunities.

Furthermore, beyond demonstrating a high degree of proficiency in waging conventional warfare, officers must, also, develop a broader cognitive basis on politics, economics, and information and communication technologies, as connected with modern warfare in a complicated and rapidly-evolving international security environment.

The Role of Interpreters and Translators in reintegration of ex-combatants

The role of interpreters and translators in peacebuilding is essential in crisis or conflict-affected areas, with regard to programs for Disarmament, Demobilization and Reintegration (DDR) for ex-combatants. The need for a more holistic, integrated approach has long been recognized but rarely achieved.

The reintegration of ex-combatants takes place in the community, and merges with development and post-conflict reconstruction. With the situation in Cameroon, there is the need for "participation" from development discourse, in order for the reintegration process to be effective in the two Anglophone regions. A participatory approach allows potential stakeholders to have a say in how interventions are conceived and implemented. Participation is largely unexplored in the context of DDR.

Participatory programs such as teaching ex-combatants two official languages, vocational training, and small business skills, which will help them quickly integrate their different communities upon return from DDR centers. Many ex-combatants are usually not adequately informed, misled into criminal activities against the country, and the development of educational and economic programs are necessary for their re-integration into the community.

Participatory programs provide opportunities for law enforcement officers to also have adequate information of what sparks the events, the role of the different actors in the conflict or crisis. More participatory processes were however noted in specific areas, such as the programs for children. But some of the constraints included short timescales for implementation, security concerns, differing agendas, and post-war disruption.

Participation proves to be a useful framework for assessing reintegration programs, and for planning the more integrated approach which has long been advocated. More participatory approaches were also linked with better program outcomes for ex-combatants, in terms of employment, relations with the community, and living conditions. They are also seen as helping to rebuild social capital, which is itself a contributory factor in terms of how participatory reintegration can support the broader objectives of peacebuilding. This wider agenda of peacebuilding, which is ultimately what DDR is supposed to be part of, is supported by a participatory approach to reintegration, and undermined by one in which there is little ownership by those directly involved.

Additionally, emerging strategic level threats increasingly require new types of attributes and career-development techniques. This, in turn, will lead to a rethinking of the balance between the necessity to engage specialists/experts, as well as to define new specific responsibilities and requirements, at all ranks: high- rank, and field- & company-grade officers. Military leaders must, on their side, determine proper balances between expertise and strategic thinking capabilities necessary for senior leadership.

Current complex international operations demand military officers who can demonstrate a clear, comprehensive, understanding of battle environment and a robust capacity to integrate capabilities in order to achieve mission success. They must comprehend both capabilities and mission objectives for units or platforms they command, as well as roles of forces from other services, allied nations, civilian government agencies, IGOs and NGOs.

Culture as a tool for civil-military relations: The U.S example

The U.S. Army War College (USAWC) defines cultural competency as the ability to understand culture as an analytical framework to facilitate strategic thinking, policy formation, and decision making. As such, it goes beyond a combination of country, region, or language specific knowledge.

In 2007 Army leadership directed the U.S. Army Training and Doctrine Command (TRADOC) G3 to serve as the executive agent in developing a service-wide solution for career continuum and pre-deployment learning about foreign cultures and languages. *The Army Culture and Foreign Language Strategy (ACFLS)* was the response. First published in December 2009, it is now being implemented as an enterprise of culture and foreign language advisors (CFLAs) and training developers positioned in many TRADOC "schoolhouses" and other training institutions to provide education in culture and language. Its evolution as a program and future efforts are detailed in the first article.

ALC 2015 affirms the "requirement for Soldiers to possess a broad foundation of learning to better prepare them to meet future challenges across the spectrum of conflict." Two of these challenges are culture and language:

"The Army operates with and among other cultures, engaging adaptive enemies where indigenous populations, varying cultures, divergent politics, and wholly different religions intersect. This requires developing Soldiers who understand that the context of the problem matters and that their understanding of the non-military world of foreign societies and cultures be

broadened. Soldiers and leaders need to learn general cultural skills that may be applied to any environment as well as just in-time information that is specific to their area of operations. The Army culture and foreign language strategy requires both career development and predeployment training to achieve the culture and foreign language capabilities necessary to conduct full-spectrum operations."

To achieve this leaders and soldiers must increase their expertise through operational experience, self-development, or as a learning opportunity through professional military education (PME) in collaboration with the Defense Language Institute Foreign Language Center (DLIFLC) and the TRADOC Culture Center (TCC), are assisting the Combined Arms Center (CAC) leadership with integrating culture and foreign language training into existing PME courses. The desired end state is to "build and sustain an Army with the right blend of culture and foreign language capabilities to facilitate full spectrum operations, now and into the future."

The ACFLS goal is to establish a baseline of CFL capabilities for all leaders and Soldiers to support the accomplishment of unit missions. The strategy's end state is to build and sustain an Army with the right blend of capabilities to facilitate full spectrum operations. The resulting force will have the ability to effectively conduct operations with and among other cultures.

CAC, at Fort Leavenworth, Kansas, was assigned the lead to implement the ACFLS in 2011 within all TRADOC organizations. As part of this implementation, CAC is working to integrate ACFLS learning objectives into existing programs of instruction (POIs) using assets (CFLAs and training developers) at the Centers of Excellence (CoEs) and other Army educational institutions using some of the basic collaborative schemas:

> Core lesson plans are provided to Initial Military Training (IMT) Command/Cadet Command/CoEs/ Command and General Staff College/U.S. Army War College/U.S. Army Sergeants Major Academy for integration into applicable POI by cohort or other appropriate applications.

> CFLAs/training developers at CoEs and schools further refine resource and curriculum requirements based on specific branch/military occupational speciality.

> The CFL Management Office (CFLMO) provides quality assurance/quality control for integrated plans to ensure standardization and synchronization.

> The Army Research Institute (ARI) and the Culture Knowledge Consortium (CKC) assist in the implementation of the enterprise with research and as a resource for materials and analytic tools as well as access to and collaboration with others of similar interests.

According to Footitt (2016), designing our 'academic hybridity in a more purposeful way' by bringing together work on translating and interpreting in danger zones by a mix of practitioners and academics, both from within and outside of Translation and Interpreting Studies and working in and outside Anglophone contexts. Which appeals on the need for Cameroon government to redefine her strategic in relation to internal wrangling.

Conclusion

This issue of Linguistica Antverpiensia is a testimony to the fact that interpreting in conflict zones is crucial and complex. The general historical overview demonstrates that interpreters and language mediators have been present during wartime throughout history. From the colonial era till date, the role of interpreters has always been essential in war-related scenarios, including negotiations and encounters or conversations of a political and conflictive nature. Although interpreters often go unnoticed, it seems clear that they have played a significant role in events and episodes throughout history.

The oppressive backdrop against which translators and interpreters work during wartime is evident. On the one hand, each translator or interpreter is ultimately an individual with a personal history, with a potentially complex, shifting and perhaps even ambivalent position in relation to different elements of the public narratives that orient the war, and often with a network of personal relations on both sides of the war. And yet translators and interpreters, like other members of society, soon find out that there is no place in war for fluid, shifting identities, for split or even strained loyalties, nor for negotiated narratives of any kind.

According to Baker (2006a) post modern assertions of the nature of identity and the status of any categories of individuals or researchers assertions that are shared a different narrative, for the fact that in war situations, and particularly for those experiencing the war firsthand, one's identity is almost completely constructed and enforced by other actors, and once constructed to suit the exigencies of war, it becomes set in stone, independent of one's actions or beliefs, with little or no room for negotiation.

Moreover, some of the most noteworthy events in the development of the modern conceptualization of the interpreting profession, such as the Paris Peace Conference and the Nuremberg Trials, took place after a period of conflict in which interpreters played a key role. One of the most interesting issues is that, despite the position the role of interpreter in conflict scenarios, no provision has been made for training interpreters specifically to work in those settings, with few exceptions. There is a need for proper training for interpreters working in conflict zones.

The Advanced School of Translator and Interpreters at the University of Buea in collaboration with the Cameroon War College, need to develop war interpreter training program. This will help provide the status of interpreters working in war scenarios and professionalize the trade. More so, the role and position of the interpreter in the communication process will be evident, the interpreting tasks to be performed, the skills needed to perform the job successfully, the type and extent of conflict-related training to be provided to interpreters, the type and extent of conflict-related duties that would be expected of the interpreter and, last but not least, issues related to ethics and neutrality.

Knowledge of history can help us identify diverse ways to approach present-day situations more critically and to offer objective insights into subjective matters that affect all the parties whether interpreters, military staff or armed forces present in the theatre of conflict. From analysis both formal and informal interpreting are crucial for an in-depth understanding of the dynamics of conflict and post conflict development. Our evidence demonstrates the fact that the current working model in development is one of informal interpreting, often provided by staff who identify themselves as development workers rather than as translators or interpreters. In both conflict and post conflict situations, interpreters at work often did not adhere to traditional notions of the interpreter as 'neutral' or as a trained professional.

Despite all, the Cameroon government set up the National Commission for the Promotion of Bilingualism and Multiculturalism in January 2017 to look at the functioning of bilingualism in Cameroon, with 15 commissioners appointed for five-year terms. However, the role of translators and interpreters are unbeatable in peacebuilding process in conflict or crisis affected areas.

On 30th March 2017, a press conference was held by the Minister of Justice and Keeper of the Seals, Laurent Esso with Presidential prescription for Anglophone lawyers. Re-affirming the existence of bi-jural system (common law and civil law) in Cameroon and a committee had been set up to examine the proposals of the Anglophone lawyers. A common law section of the Supreme Court is to be established so that cases can be heard in English and in compliance with the common law where necessary, with a review of the number of judges available to hear those cases.

The level of Higher Education, a Faculty of Legal and Political Sciences is to be established at the University of Buea, as well as departments of English Law at a number of universities. Training will be made available for English speaking judges and legal officers. Recruitment of a larger number of Anglophone teachers for judicial and legal training is planned and the setting up of a common law section at the training school. While waiting for the training to be implemented and undertaken, recruitment of interpreters to provide services at courts will take place.

Upon the numerous recommendations in relation to respecting the law and due process in respect of the legal violations that have been committed, a request for the Minister of Defense to examine favorably the possibility of ending judicial procedures before the Military Tribunal against persons arrested in connection with the crisis.

REFERENCES

Ali, H. I. H., Alhassan, A.m & Burma, I. (2019). An investigation into the interpreters' challenges in conflict zones: The case of Darfur region in Sudan. Arab World English Journal for Translation & Literary Studies, 3 (3) 37-50.

Amich, M. G. (2013). The vital role of conflict interpreters. Nawa Journal of Language and Communication 7 (2), 15-26.

AIIC 2012. Code of Professional Ethics [online]. Available from: http://aiic.net/page/6724/

AIIC 2013. Conflict Zone Field Guide [online]. http://aiic.net/page/3853/aiic-red-t-and-fit-introduce-the-first-conflict-zone-field-guide-lang/1

Ayasrah, B. (2015) The Role of Translation in Shaping Media and Political Discourses in Times of Conflict: The Syrian "Spring" in Context. Thesis submitted in fulfillment of the requirements for the degree of doctor of philosophy. Faculty of Social Sciences & Humanities (FSSH) London Metropolitan University

Abbadi, R. (2014) 'The Construction of Arguments in English and Arabic: A Comparison of the Linguistic Strategies Employed in Editorials', Argumentum 10, pp. 724-746.

Abdul-Fattah, H. (2011) 'A Formal-Functional Analysis of the English Modal Auxiliaries', Jordan Journal of Modern Languages and Literature (JJMLL) Vol. 3, No.1, pp. 39-63.

Baker, M. (1992/ revised edition 2011) In Other Words: A Course book on Translation, London and New York: Routledge.

Baker, M. (1993) 'Corpus Linguistics and Translation Studies: Implications and Applications' In M.

Baker, G. Francis and E. Tognini-Bonelli (eds.), Text and Technology: In Honour of John Sinclair, Amsterdam and Philadelphia: John Benjamins, pp. 233-250.

Baker, M. (1995) 'Corpora in Translation Studies: An Overview and Some Suggestions for Future Research', Target, 7: 2, pp. 223-243.

Baker, M. (1996) 'Corpus-Based Translation Studies: The Challenges that Lie Ahead'. In Somers, H. (ed.) Terminology, LSP and Translation: Studies in Language Engineering, in Honour of Juan C. Sager. Amsterdam and Philadelphia: John Benjamins Publishing, pp. 175-186.

Baker, M. (1998) 'Introduction' In M. Baker (ed.) Routledge Encyclopedia of Translation Studies, London and New York: Routledge.

Baker, M. (1999) 'The Role of Corpora in Investigating the Linguistic Behaviour of Professional Translators', International Journal of Corpus Linguistics, 4, pp. 281-298.

Baker, M. (2001) 'The Pragmatics of Cross-Cultural Contact and Some False Dichotomies in Translation Studies'. In M. Olohan, CTIS Occasional Papers. Vol. 1, UMIST, Manchester: Centre for Translation and Intercultural Studies, pp.7-20.

Baker, M. (2004) 'A Corpus-based View of Similarity and Difference in Translation', International

Journal of Corpus Linguistics, 9 (2), pp. 167-193.

Baker, M. (2006a) Translation and Conflict: A Narrative Account. Routledge.

Baker, M. (2006b) 'Contextualization in Translator- and Interpreter-Mediated Events', Journal of Pragmatics 38, (3), pp. 321-337.

Baker, M. (2007) 'Reframing Conflict in Translation', Social Semiotics, 17 (2), pp. 151-169.

Baker, M. (2008) 'Ethics of Renarration: Mona Baker is interviewed by Andrew Chesterman'.Cultus1 (1), pp. 10-33.

Baker, M. (2009) Resisting State Terror: Theorising Communities of Activist Translators andInterpreters'. In E. Bielsa and C. Hughes (eds.) Globalisation, Political Violence and Translation, Basingstoke: Palgrave Macmillan, pp. 222-242.

Baker, M. (2010) 'Interpreters and translators in the war zone: Narrated and narrators'. In M.

Baker, M. and Maier, C. (2011) 'Ethics in Interpreter and Translator Training: Critical Perspectives'.The Interpreter and Translator Trainer 5 (1), pp. 1-14.

Bakker, M., Koster, C. and Van Leuven-Zwart, K. (1998) 'Shifts of Translation'. In M. Baker and K. Malmakjaer, (eds.). Routledge Encyclopaedia of Translation Studies, London, New York

Baigorri-Jalón, J., 2000. La interpretación de conferencias: el nacimiento de una profesión. De París a Nuremberg. Granada: Comares.

Bartolini, G., 2010. General Principles of International Humanitarian Law [online seminar aiic.net 9 March]

Biddle, F. (1947). The Nuremberg Trial. American Philosophical Society Proceedings,91(3), 294.

C. FERAUD, Les interprètes de l'armée d'Afrique, alger, 1876.

Christine Chinkin, Comment, Due Process and Witness Anonymity, 91 AM. J. INT'L L. 75, 75 (1997).

Cronin, M., 2002. The Empire talks back: orality, heteronomy and the cultural turn in interpreting studies. In F. Pochhacker and M. Shlesinger, eds. The Interpreting Studies Reader. London: Routledge, 387-397.

Catford, C. (1965) A Linguistic Theory of Translation: An Essay in Applied Linguistics. London: Oxford University Press. outledge, pp. 226- 231.

M. DRAGOVIC-DROUET, "The Practice of Translation and Interpreting During the Conflicts in The Former Yugoslavia (1991-1999)"

Inghilleri and S. Harding (eds.). The Translator, 16 (2), Special Issue: Translation and Violent Conflict, pp. 197-222.

E. ELIAS-BURSAC, Translating Evidence and Interpreting Testimony at a War Crimes Tribunal: Working in a Tug-of-War, Plagrave, 2015.

European Commission. (2012). Studies on translation and multilingualism. Luxemburg: Publications Office of the European Union.

F. FERRACCI, Gli interpreti in zone di conflitto: il caso dei civili afgani al servizio degli Stati Uniti, Ma Degree Final Thesis, 2017, Università degli Studi Internazionali Di Roma.

Fitchett, L., 2012. The AIIC project to help interpreters in conflict areas. In: H. Footitt and M. Kelly, eds. Languages and the Military. Alliances, Occupation and Peace Building. Basingstoke: Palgrave Macmillan, 175-185.

Footitt, H., 2016. War and Culture Studies in 2016: Putting 'Translation' into the Transnational? Journal of War & Culture Studies, 9 (3), 209–221.

Footitt, H., and Kelly, M., eds., 2012a. Languages and the Military: Alliances, Occupation and Peace Building. Basingstoke: Palgrave Macmillan.

Footitt, H., and Kelly, M., 2012b. Languages at War. Policies and Practices of Language Contacts in Conflict. Basingstoke: Palgrave Macmillan.

Fonkenmun, E. L. (2007). The Importance of the Mastery of the Subject Field in   the Translation of Legal Documents: A Case Study of the Cameroon Penal Code. Unpublished M.A Thesis in Translation, ASTI, University of   Buea.

FRANCESCA GAIBA, THE ORIGINS OF SIMULTANEOUS INTERPRETATION: THE NUREMBERG TRIAL 110 (1998).

Gaiba, F. (1998). History of interpreting: Interpretation at the Nuremberg Trial. Ottawa, ON: University of Ottawa Press.

G. Bartolini, Contractors as "Persons who Accompany the Armed Forces", in F. FRANCIONI-N. RONZITTI (ed.), War by Contract. Human Rights, Humanitarian Law, and Private

Contractors, oxford, 2011, p. 219 et seq.; Pictet (ed.), The Geneva Conventions, cit., pp. 64-65.

G. SLUITER, Appearance of Witness and Unavailability of Subpoena Powers for the Court, in R. Bellelli (ed.), International Criminal Justice. Law and Practice from the Rome Statute and Its Review, Burlington, 2010, p. 459 et seq.

Giulio Bartolini and Francesco Ferracci. INTERPRETERS IN CONFLICT ZONES: AN INTERNATIONAL LEGAL ASSESSMENT

Hardman, D. (2008) Political Ideology and Identity in British Newspaper Discourse. Unpublished PHD thesis, University of Nottingham.

HILARY GASKIN, EYEWITNESSES AT NUREMBERG 47 (1990)

ICTY, Trial Chamber, Prosecutor v. Delalic and Others, Decision on the Motion Ex Parte concerning the Issue of a Subpoena to an Interpreter, July 8, 1997, paragraphs 18-20.

ICTY, appeals Chamber, Brdjanin and Talic, Decision on Interlocutory Appeal, 11 december 2002. on these issues see M.A. FAIRLIE, Evidentiary Privilege of Journalists Reporting in Areas of Armed Conflict, in American Journal of International Law, 2004, p. 805 et seq.

ICRC, Interpretative Guidance on the Notion of Direct Participation in Hostilities under International Humanitarian Law, Geneva, 2009, pp. 27-36.

Inghilleri, M. (2009) 'Translators in War Zones: Ethics under Fire in Iraq'. In E. Bielsa and C. Hughes: Globalisation, Political Violence and Translation, Houndsmills (eds.), Palgrave Macmillan.

Inghilleri, M. (2010) 'You Don't Make War Without Knowing Why: The Decision to Interpret in Iraq'. In M. Inghilleri and S. Harding (eds.). The Translator, 16 (2), Special Issue: Translation and Violent Conflict, pp. 175-196.

Inghilleri, M. and Harding, S. (2010) 'Translating Violent Conflict'. In M. Inghilleri and S. Harding (eds.). The Translator, 16 (2), Special Issue: Translation and Violent Conflict, pp. 165-173.

Jägar, S. (2001) 'Discourse and Knowledge: Theoretical and Methodological Aspects of a Critical Discourse and Dispositive Analysis'. In R. Wodak and M. Meyer (eds.) Methods of Critical Discourse Analysis, London: Sage. pp. 32-62.

J. MCDOWELL, The International Committee of the Red Cross as a Witness before International Criminal Tribunals, in Chinese Journal of International Law, 2002, p. 158 et seq.

Julie A. House (2014) Conference Interpretation in The Military Environment of Francophone West Africa

J.P. LAWRENCE, US plan to fix visa delays for interpreters who helped troops deemed 'offensive', in Stars and Stripes, march 12, 2020 <https://www.stripes.com/news/us-plan-to-fix-visa-delays-forinterpreters-who-helped-troops-deemed-offensive-1.622149>.

J.R. ELTING, Swords around a Throne. Napoleon's Grande Armée, New York, 1988, pp. 93-94.

Joshua Karton (2018) Lost in Translation: International Criminal Tribunals and the Legal Implications of Interpreted Testimony. Vanderbilt Journal of Transnational Law

J.C. Randal, Preserving the Fruits of Ethnic Cleansing: Bosnian Serbs, Expulsion Victims See Process as Beyond Reversal, in The Washington Post, February 11, 1993.

J. Pictet (ed.). The Geneva Conventions of 12 August 1949: Commentary, vol. iii, Geneva, 1960, p. 487.

JUNGWHA, C. (2003) "The Interpretive Theory of Translation and Its Current Applications," Interpretation Studies, No. 3, December 2003, pages 1-15. Available at:http://jaits.jpn.org/home/kaishi2003/pdf/01-choi_final_.pdf [Consulted on 10 Mar 2014].

K. DOUGHTY, Language and International Criminal Justice in Africa: Interpretation at the ICTR, in International Journal of Transitional Justice, 2017, 239 et seq.

Kelly, M., and Baker, C., 2013. Interpreting the Peace. Peace Operations, Conflict and Language in Bosnia-Herzegovina. Basingstoke: Palgrave Macmillan.

Kujamäki, P., and Footitt, H., 2019. Military History and Translation Studies: Shifting Territories, Uneasy Borders. In M. Kelly, H.Footitt and M. Salama-Carr, eds. The Palgrave Handbook of Languages and Conflict. Cham: Palgrave Macmillan, 113–136.

L. FITCHETT, Hearing on Interpreters in Conflict Zones in the European Parliament, february 19, 2018.

L. Ruiz Rosendo and C. Persaud, "interpreters and interpreting in Conflict Zones and scenarios: a historical perspective", in Linguistica Antverpiensia, New Series – Themes in Translation Studies, 2016, 15: 1-35.

L. Ruiz Rosendo and M. Barea MuñoZ, "Towards a typology of interpreters in war-related scenarios in the Middle East", in Translation Spaces 6:2, 2017, pp. 182-208

Lefevere, A. (1992) Translation, Rewriting and the Manipulation of Literary Fame, London and New York: Routledge.

Lefevere, A. (1993) Translating Literature: Practice and Theory in a Comparative Literature Context. New York: The Modern Language Association of America.

Lewis, J., 2012. Languages at War: a UK Military of Defence Perspective. In: H. Footitt and M. Kelly, eds. Languages and the Military. Alliances, Occupation and Peace Building. Basingstoke: Palgrave Macmillan, 58-69.

Mona Baker (2010) Narratives of terrorism and security: 'accurate' translations, suspicious frames, Critical Studies on Terrorism, 3:3, 347-364, DOI:10.1080/17539153.2010.521639

Marais, K., 2014. Translation Theory and Development Studies: A Complexity Theory Approach. New York and Abingdon: Routledge.

Mairs, R. (2011). Translator, traditor: The interpreter as traitor in classical tradition. Greece & Rome, 58, 64–81. doi:10.1017/S0017383510000537.

Mattingly, G. (1937). The first resident embassies: Mediaeval Italian origins of modern diplomacy. Speculum, 12, 423–439. doi:10.2307/2849298.

Maitland, S. (2017). What is cultural translation? London, England: Bloomsbury Academic.

Moreno-Bello, Y. (2021). Narratives in conflict and the limits on the interpreter's agency: A case study from the UN Peacekeeping mission in Lebanon. Linguistica Antverpiensia, New Series: Themes in Translation Studies, 20, 94–114.

Moser-Mercer, B., & Bali, G. (2008). Interpreting in zones of crisis and war: AIIC.Retrieved from http://aiic.net/page/2979/interpreting-in-zones-of-crisis-andwar/lang/1.

Munday, J. (2014). Using primary sources to produce a microhistory of translation and translators: theoretical and methodological concerns.

Neba, W. T., & Amos, N. M. A. (2019) Ascertaining The Quality of the Translated Version of the New Cameroon Penal Code. Advances in Social Sciences Research Journal, 6(4) 7-21.

Office of the Assistant Secretary of Defense for Logistics & Materiel readiness, Contractor Support of U.S. Operation in the USCENTCOM Area of Responsibility, 2nd quarter FY2020, April 2020. <https://www.acq.osd.mil/log/ps/.CentCom_reports.html/5a_april_2020.pdf>.

P. SNELLMAN, "Constraints on and dimensions of military interpreter neutrality", Linguistica Antverpiensia, New Series: Themes in Translation Studies, 2016, 15, pp. 60-281.

Pérez, M. (2007) 'Translating Conflict: Advertising in a Globalised Era'. In M. Salama-Carr (ed.) Translating and Interpreting

Conflict: Approaches to Translation Studies, Amsterdam: Rodopi, pp.149-168.

Prosecutor v. Tadic, Case No. IT-94-1-T, Transcript, at 47 (May 7, 1996), available at http://www.un.org/icty/transe1/960507IT. htm [hereinafter Tadic Transcript].

Pym, A. (1998) Methods in Translation History, Manchester: St. Jerome.

Pym, A. (2001a) 'Introduction', The Return to Ethics in Translation Studies (ed.), Special Issue, The Translator. Vol. 7, No. 2, 129-138.

Pym, A. (2001b) The Return to Ethics in Translation Studies (ed.), Special Issue of the Translator.Vol. 7, No. 2.

R.S. LEE (ed.), The International Criminal Court. Elements of Crimes and Rules of Procedure and Evidence, New York, 2001, p. 360.

Rafael, V. (2010) 'Translation in wartime', in M. Baker (ed.) Critical Readings in Translation Studies, pp. 383-390.

Rafael, V. 2012. 'Translation and the US Empire. Counterinsurgency and the resistance of language'. The Translator, 18 (1): 1-22

Rosendo, L. R., and Persaud, C., eds., 2016. Interpreting in conflict situations and in conflict zones throughout history. Special Issue of Linguistica Antverpiensia, New Series, 15.

Salama-Carr, M., ed., 2007. Translating and Interpreting Conflict, Amsterdam and New York: Rodopi.

S. JEANNET, Recognition of the ICRC's Long-Standing Rule of Confidentiality: An Important Decision by the International Criminal Tribunal for the Former Yugoslavia, in International Review of the Red Cross, 2000, p. 403 et seq.

S. TRESCHEL, Human Rights in Criminal Proceedings, Coll. Courses Ac. Eur. Law, oxford, 2005, pp.327-339.

Schäffner, C. (2002) The Role of Discourse Analysis for Translation and in Translation Training.UK: Multilingual Matters Ltd.

Schäffner, C. (2003) Third Ways and New Centers: Ideological Unity or Difference? In M. Calzade-Péreze. Apropos of Ideology: Translation Studies on Ideology- Ideology in Translation Studies, Manchester: St. Jerome, pp. 23-41.

Snellman, P. (2014). The agency of military interpreters in Finnish crisis management operations (Master's thesis, University of Tampere). Retrieved from http://urn.fi/URN:NBN:fi:uta-201403061187.

Stahuljak, Z. (2009) 'War, Translation, Translationism: Interpreters in and of the War (Croatia 1991-1992)', in M. Baker (ed.) Critical Readings in Translation Studies, pp. 391-414.

Stolze, R. (2013). "The Legal Translator's approach to Texts" in Humanities 2013, 2. pp. 56-71.

Taylor, T. (1955). The Nuremberg trials. Columbia Law Review, 55, 488–525.doi:10.2307/1119814.

Tchoungui, G. (1983). "Focus on official bilingualism in Cameroon: its relationship to   education". In Koenig, E. et   al (eds.), 93-115.

Tesseur, W. and Footitt, H. (2019) Professionalisms at war? Interpreting in conflict and post-conflict situations. Journal of War & Culture Studies, 12 (3). pp. 268-284. ISSN 1752-6272 doi: https://doi.org/10.1080/17526272.2019.1644415 https://centaur.reading.ac.uk/85317/

Tesseur, W., ed., 2018. Researching translation and interpreting in Non-Governmental Organisations. Special issue of Translation Spaces, 7(1).

Toury, G. (1980b) 'The Translator as a Non-conformist to be, or: How to Train Translators so as to Violate Translational Norms'. In S. Poulsen, & W. Wilss (eds.), pp. 180-194.

TRADOC, 2006. Arab Cultural Awareness 58 Factsheets. Handbook no.2, office of the Deputy Chief of Staff for Intelligence US Army Training and Doctrine Command, Ft. Leavenworth, Kansas.

UN General Assembly, Model Status-of-Forces Agreement for Peace-Keeping Operations, october 9, 1990, UN Doc. a/45/594.

Wong, D. & Shen, D. (1999). Factors Influencing the Process of Translating. Meta, 44(1), 78–100. https://doi.org/10.7202/004616ar

Wright, K., 2015. Using local field staff as interpreters [online]. Available from: http://odihpn.org/resource/interpreter-guidelines/

OTHERS

Jodie Blackstock (2017) TRIAL OBSERVATION REPORT. Nkongo Felix Agbor-Balla and Others Cameroon. Bar Human Rights Committee

2009 Army Posture Statement, Interpreter/Translator Program, available at: http://www.army.mil/aps/09/information_papers/interpreter_translator_program.html

DefenseLanguage Institute Foreign Language Center website:http://www.dliflc.edu/index.html

"Lend Me Your Ears: US Military Turns to Contractor Linguists" Defense Industry Daily, August 22, 2013:http://www.defenseindustrydaily.com/lend-me-your-ears-us-militaryturns-to-contractor-linguists-05934/scriba el TEXTO (Calibri 12 - justificado), a partir de aquí…..

Human Rights Committee, General Comment 29, States of Emergency (article 4), UN Doc. CCPR/C/21/Rev.1/Add.11(2001), para7.

CRTV, 'SCNC and the Cameroon Anglophone Civil Society Consortium banned,'18th January 2017, http://crtv.cm/fr/latest-news/top-news-24/scnc-and-the-cameroon-anglophone-civil-society-consortiumbanned--18545.htm

CRTV, 'The Anglophone crisis: three front runners brought to trial,' 2nd February 2017,http://crtv.cm/fr/latest-news/top-news-24/the-anglophone-crisis-three-front-runners-brought-to-trial-18624.htm

STV, 'Lawyer Dr Nkongho Felix Agbor Balla discusses issues leading to strike', 29th November 2016, available on https://www.youtube.com/watch?v=02QAoz2rQnA

Special Rapporteur on human rights and counter-terrorism: UN Doc. E/CN.4/2006/98(2005), para 46.

HRC General Comment No. 32, Article 14: Right to equality before courts and tribunals and to a fair trial, UN Doc CCPR/C/GC/32 2007) at 33.

ACHPR, 'Press Release on the Human Rights Situation in Cameroon Following strike actions of Lawyers, Teachers and Civil Society', 12th December 2016.

Africa Times, 'Cameroon citizens join lawyers' protest in streets of Bamenda,' 8th November 2016, available at, http://africatimes.com/2016/11/08/cameroon-citizens-join-lawyers-protest-in-streets-of-bamenda/

Cameroon Concord, 'Cameroon: Common Law Lawyers Storm the Premises of Bamenda Court,' available at, http://cameroon-concord.com/headlines/item/7252-cameroon-common-law-lawyers-storm-the-premisesof-bamenda-court;

All Africa, 'Cameroon: Bilingualism, Multiculturalism-Commission Begins Work Tomorrow,'26th April 2017, available at http://allafrica.com/stories/201704260689.html

UN Doc CAT/C/CMR/CO/4, Concluding observations of the Committee against Tortureon Cameroon, 19 May 2010, at [15].

NCHRF, Observation and investigation mission of the NCHRF in connection with case of human rights violations during the strike actions in the North West and South West regions, 1-4 February 2017, available at,http://www.cndhl.cm/index.php/repository/func-startdown/42/

Case 266/2003 Kevin Mgwanga Gunme et al/Cameroon, 45th Ordinary Session, African Commission, EX.CL/529(XV) 13-27 May, 2009, http://old.achpr.org/english/Decison_Communication/Cameroon/Comm.%20266-03.pdf

FrontlineDefenders,https://www.frontlinedefenders.org/en/case/ nkongho-felix-agbor-balla-detainedand-charged-military-court-eight-counts

Amnesty International, 'Cameroon: Arrests and Civil Society Bans Risk Inflaming Tensions in English-Speaking Regions, 20th January 2017', https://www.amnesty.org/en/press releases/2017/01/cameroon-arrests-and-civil-society-bans-risk inflaming-tensions-in-english-speaking-regions/

All Africa Network, 'Breaking news!!!: Mancho Bibixy arrested in Bamenda Northwest Cameroon,' 19th January 2017, http://www.alafnet.com/breaking-news-mancho-bibixy-arrested-in-bamenda-northwestcameroon/

The Commonwealth, http://thecommonwealth.org/our-member-countries/cameroon/history

http://thecommonwealth.org/our-member-countries/cameroon/ constitution-politics

http://www.globalsecurity.org/military/world/africa/cm-political-parties.htm

ABOUT THE AUTHOR

SARON MESSEMBE Obia is a figure of distinction in the field of international security. He studied Criminology and Security Management (PGD) and Security Studies (MSc) at the Pan African Institute for Development West Africa- PAID-WA, and is a Certified Public Policy Analyst at the Nkafu Policy Institute. He is a counter terrorism analyst of Islamic Theology of Counter Terrorism-ITCT, a UK based Counter Islamist Terrorism Think Tank. He worked with the International Association for Counter Terrorism and Security Professional South East Asia-IACSP SEA, as Assistant Editor and IACSP SEA Representative for Cameroon Publication Division. He is the author of numerous books, including: '*The Criminal Mind In The Age Of Globalization*', '*Jihadist Tendencies in West Africa Boko Haram's Game – Yesterday, Today and Tomorrow*', and '*Weaponized Drones Terrorism in Africa Al Qeada, Al Shabaab, Boko Haram & ISIS*'.

www.ingramcontent.com/pod-product-compliance
Lightning Source LLC
LaVergne TN
LVHW051552170726
843492LV00006B/2057